"Julie Olsen is the mentor we all wish we had...giving priceless advice that we all need. And now it's here! Keep this book by your side as you navigate career transition, career change and career success."

Vanessa Van Edwards, Best Selling Author of Captivate: The Science of Succeeding with People & founder at <u>Science of People</u>

"Dr. Julie Olsen has written a must-read for anyone currently facing or even considering a career transition. Her real-life experience and academic expertise make her an authority on the topic. As someone who recently navigated a career transition, I can attest that the principles Dr. Olsen highlights in *That Would Have Been Nice to Know!* are both on point and practical. Read this book - and learn from one of the best."

Dr. Joe Pennino, Chief, Roswell Fire Department, Roswell, GA

"Captivating, entertaining, and educational. As a recently retired military member, *That Would Have Been Nice to Know* would have been helpful. Thankfully, many friends reached out and provided advice along the way. But, to have it all in one place with testimonial and no-frills teaching points and perspective from different points of view is invaluable. The entire book is a must read but I particularly connected with Chapter 6, which should be required reading for all transition military members. This book is not a recipe but a thought-provoking analysis which provides the tools to navigate the unknown as each situation and environment can be vastly different. Thank you, Dr. Olsen, for taking the time to take a complex topic, giving it order, and making it enjoyable to read."

Colonel Jose Aguilar, US Army (Ret.)

"What a relevant perspective to bring to the working world! In her book, Dr. Olsen talks about building a 'healthy mind' which is difficult to maintain during career transitions. Personally, I see the difficulty of students transitioning from learning academics to understanding the realities of their chosen profession. This difficult challenge is covered in the first chapter, and then Dr. Olsen carefully covers the other transitions that are often unplanned in one's career trajectory. This book is modern and relatable to professionals in every industry."

Michelle "Molly" Keating, Ed.D., Director of Career Services, South University

"This is the book I wish I had and heeded the advice when I was just starting my career. Of course, when I was 20, I already knew everything. Or so I arrogantly thought. Over the next five decades, I slowly learned the lessons in this book. The old adage 'experience is the best teacher,' is a lie. The best teacher is someone else's experience. As Eleanor Roosevelt famously said 'learn from the mistakes of others. You can't possibly live long enough to make them all yourself.' Do yourself a favor. Read this book and take the lessons to heart. You will reach your goals decades sooner if you follow this book's advice."

H. Roy Austin, CPA, CMA, MBA, Rockwell Business Solutions and author of The Alligator Business Solution.

"In this book, Dr. Olsen takes a very complex idea or a subject, gets other folks' opinions on it, and brings them into one collective space. Right now, we're seeing quite a bit of career movement, whether it is people moving from one company to another, or perhaps people moving from one career to another, or simply taking that next career step. This book shares all things that people need to know as they embark on that next journey. It's the information you need to make great decisions and succeed."

Rollis Fontenot III, HR Maximizer, Founder & Chief Innovation Officer

"Julie Olsen's *That Would Have Been Nice to Know!* is a great example of what happens when insight meets action. Whether you are fresh out of college, headed to retirement, or somewhere in between, this book offers real-world stories and practical strategies for navigating career transitions. Everyone from leaders to new hires can benefit from Dr. Olsen's concepts and take-a-ways for conquering those inevitable challenges of change."

Dr. Carmita McCall, CEO, Impact Social Solutions

"Dr. Olsen captures uplifting realism universally applicable for everyone. The stories and work-life applications will serve as a field guide for career transitions. Reflections and action plans really make it about you. You will build a mirrored relationship with each interview. It WILL influence you, motivate you, and have you reflecting...ultimately wanting to share your discoveries with others."

Frank Gonzalez IV, Lifelong People Enthusiast

"This book is the ultimate guide on how to stay relevant and be a meaningful contributor even as the world changes. I highly recommend for everyone at any stage of their life."

Jonathan Small, VP of Human Resources

"Within these pages are practical tips for inexperienced and seasoned professionals who are navigating new positions, roles, and/or career moves. *That Would Have Been Nice to Know!* will position you to not only succeed at your current job but to excel in your profession. The real-world stories and lessons about career beginnings, transitions, and fails offers the reader a comforting glimpse into the thoughts and actions of real people seeking to find their footing and stride in their career. Dr. Olsen's advice is encouraging and puts a positive spin on working through challenging work issues and environments."

Dr. Latoya James

"Julie Olsen's compelling book, *That Would Have Been Nice to Know!*, is a must read for anyone contemplating a career transition. The stories and life lessons from those who lived through tough transitions are invaluable to avoid the same pitfalls, disappointment, and wasted time in the wrong place. And CEOs and Managers – this book gives insight to what employees experience after a transition into a new career or a promotion, and to what they need from the leadership team to be successful."

Mary J Nestor, Founder, MJN Consulting; Speaker, Consultant, Coach
Best-selling Author, "Say It Now! Say It Right! How
to Handle Tough and Tender Conversations"

THAT WOULD HAVE BEEN HAVE BEEN NICE TO KNOW!

Advice From Those Who Made Successful Career Transitions.

DR. JULIE A. OLSEN

That Would Have Been Nice to Know!
Advice From Those Who Made Successful Career Transitions
by Dr. Julie Olsen

P.O. Box 30075
Savannah, Ga. 31410
www.workplaceadvancement.com

ISBN: 978-1-7374922-0-7

CONTENTS

DEDICATION

To my amazing husband, Bill Cathcart, who supported me through my recent career transition and encouraged me to write this book. In addition to assisting me with securing interviews with interesting people, he served as my initial editor. Thanks for giving me the quiet time needed to organize and capture my thoughts on paper and for loving me enough to give up some of our time together so this book could become a reality.

FOREWORD

I appreciate people who are curious. People who are curious about intellectual concepts and their application. Curious about making sense of the world. Curious about people. It is one of the traits I value most when deciding if a colleague will become a friend. A colleague is someone I work with, who has some of the same methodologies and types of business in common with me. A friend is someone that takes curiosity to a new level, and cares about what they find out about. A friend shares in the learning journey.

Julie is a friend. She learns more than she needs to learn so her understanding of a concept is deep. Her natural curiosity makes her keep digging. She inhales concepts and exhales new and better concepts. In that way, she creates new ways of thinking and new ways of helping others. Her book, *That Would Have Been Nice to Know*, is a natural culmination of that process. In it, she has taken curiosity to a new level. The outcome is brilliant.

What is brilliant about the book? Julie took her natural curiosity and put it to work. She interviews several people who were at different points in their careers and different stages in their life. There are people who have just begun the journey, and those who are closer to the end. She asks probing questions. She follows where her curiosity leads her. She tells their stories respectfully. She is able to share takeaways with her readers that make sense. For the people who peruse these pages, the time will be well spent. Internalizing the ideas will be revelatory, no matter the place in life's journey one is.

The book made me think of is the old story about the three bricklayers. Someone asked three bricklayers, "What are you doing?" The first one replied "I am laying bricks." The second one said: "I am building a church." The third one said: "I am building a cathedral to glorify God." My take on the story? The first person has a job, the second has a career, and the third one has a calling. The difference is that a job sustains income, a career sustains intellect, but a calling sustains life. The book includes the examples of all three phases and how a job becomes a calling.

And that may be the most brilliant part of all.

Chip Scholz, Certified Business Coach,
Scholz and Associates, Inc.

INTRODUCTION

"You want me to do what?" Those were the words I spoke when I was asked to run the Psychiatric Care Unit at a major level one trauma center. Nothing in my past would even indicate that I was outwardly qualified for the position. Why were they asking me to take on the challenge? Let's take a look at my background and see what the hospital leadership was seeing.

After completing my MBA and working eight years as a director of a YMCA, I accepted a position as a leadership development trainer at a regional trauma center. In this role, I would be able to use my academic and real-world leadership experience to help develop leaders, which had become my passion. A little more than two years into that role, I mentioned to the vice president of human resources that I would be open to a new challenge, if there was one that fit my skills, and where I could contribute to the organization at a greater level. Although I had no clear plan, I felt I could add more value.

About a year later, the organization fell on difficult times, and the decision was made to reduce staff. Every employee who did not "touch the patient" became concerned about their job. And that included me. Then, in just one day, more than 150 positions were eliminated. We were stunned and hoped it was over. Those of us who did not "have the talk" thought we were safe.

The next morning when I arrived at work, I was summoned to the office of the vice president of patient care. We had a leadership workshop planned for 25 of her leaders, so I grabbed my folder and headed over. I assumed that perhaps she wanted to make a few changes to the topics due to recent events. As I walked into the office, there sat not only the VP of patient care, but also, unexpectedly, the VP of human resources, the same two women who had conducted many difficult conversations the day before! Instinctively, I decided that I was there to be laid off and felt panic.

Summoning my resolve, I looked at the two ladies and said, "I'm sorry, I didn't know that was what this meeting is about. I didn't bring my employee badge." The two ladies laughed and said, "Well, that's not what this is about. You are not about to be laid off." "Then you better get to the point quick," I replied. The VP of patient care looked at me and said, "OK, we want you to run our psychiatric care unit." I laughed and responded, "No, really, why am I here?"

They were telling the truth. These two ladies saw something in me that was a good match for the job, but I did not know what it could be. To be honest, running a psychiatric hospital was never on my dream jobs list! Along with not being certain about how to even spell "psychiatric," I certainly did not know where to start as the leader of the unit. As part of their "sell" job, the two VPs shared that the service was losing millions of dollars each year, and if I could not find a way to turn it around, the service would be closed. Wow, no pressure there! I, of course, accepted the leadership challenge.

During the next two years working in the psychiatric field, I had many adventures. I met the bomb squad when they found a suspicious package by my car (it turned out to be a typewriter in a metal case, who knew?). I met the SWAT team when a man walked in with a gun and proclaimed that he was going to kill himself, and I had my life threatened by an anonymous caller.

Although all of that rose my adrenalin level, and were rare events even for a psychiatric facility, I learned, and grew, so much during those two years. I learned about people and their real challenges, the desperate need for community mental health services, a new way to lead people during significant change, and how to navigate a very complicated insurance payment system.

Having now experienced transitions from education to the career world, from a small nonprofit that builds healthy minds and bodies, to a large nonprofit healthcare system, and from a role as a leadership trainer to running a trauma center's major service line, I realized often limited resources and little time was spent on preparing people for their career transitions. There are many people, like me, who move into new roles and struggle with new expectations. Many respond by doing the same things they did in their previous roles, assuming the organization knows what they need and will provide the necessary resources, or worse yet, become functionally paralyzed from lack of direction, while waiting for instructions from their manager. Needless to say, these strategies do not work well! Most organizations hire you for your expertise; however, they may not be sure what you actually do know, where you may be confused, or what is unclear.

The failure in career transitions is when people accept a new role without fully considering their personal strengths and the needs of the new role, and then rely totally on the organization to provide the necessary tools for success. Unfortunately, this strategy can lead to a bad job fit, or to new employees or leaders conducting themselves in a manner that can ultimately undermine their success.

Case in point, I remember working with one leader who moved from being a successful executive in the for-profit sector to the CEO of a nonprofit organization. She relied too heavily on the skills that made her successful in the for-profit arena and failed to fully understand, among other things, how to effectively work with a board of directors.

Ultimately, this oversight led to her recognizing her lack of needed adaption and new skills far too late, and unfortunately, the need to find a new role elsewhere.

I have come to realize that career transitions are not successful because of what the organization does, but by means of personal accountability. Instead of jumping into the new role simply with an optimistic attitude and a reliance on previous successes, you will need to take personal responsibility to learn the new organization, the new role, the adaptations needed to your style, and the new skills necessary to succeed.

While working with my healthcare organization, I recall assisting a new leader who moved from a technical role into a leadership role. He struggled at first, relying heavily on his technical skills. When he realized he was having difficulty as a leader, he contacted me for help. We identified the skills needed to be successful in his new role, specifically which previous skills needed to take a lesser role, and the mindset shifts he needed to make. He sought out a mentor, became a student of leadership, studied the organizational culture, and ultimately rose to the level of vice president. Using the experiences of people in many different industries, this book will provide insight into several transitions experienced by people who went before you, their lessons learned, and their advice for you as you go about achieving a successful transition.

Throughout their lifetime, most Americans spend more than 90,000 hours at work. According to Gina Belli at PayScale, during that time, they will have an average of 12 job changes. If you make it to five years with an employer, you have stayed longer with one employer than most Americans! In fact, the Bureau of Labor Statistics indicates that the median number of years a typical employee stays with a company is 4.2 years.

There has been a lot of research on why people leave a job, with the results ranging from expanding their experience or increasing earning potential, to discovering the job was not a good fit, or that they simply wanted a greater challenge. If you have recently made a career change or are planning one in the future, you need to consider what will be different in your new role, how the changes may impact your preparation and skills, and how you may need to adapt to be successful.

This book goes beyond the job search and provides tools and tips on how to be successful as you transition into a new role. According to author Jeff Hyman, in his Forbes article, *The Number One Reason People Fail In New Roles (It's Not What You Think),* 46% of new hires failed within 18 months. Building on my experience and knowledge gained from years of consulting with people at various stages in their careers, I have found there are a great number of books on how to look for and secure a new job, but books on how to transition and succeed in your new role are not as prolific.

This book shares experiences, sometimes humorous, from people who have made successful transitions, while providing tips and resources for people who are about to, or are newly experiencing, a career transition. Whether this is your first transition from college to the professional arena, or you are changing positions in the same organization, switching organizations or business sectors entirely, or even experiencing other transitions throughout the career life cycle, this book will provide you with valuable insight.

That Would Have Been Nice to Know! addresses fundamental questions regarding the mindset changes that need to happen to be successful in a new and different role. The primary purpose of this book is help people prepare for and to be successful navigating simple or complex career transitions. Each chapter will start with an introduction of people who have experience in the change that is being addressed, move to the common themes that arose during their experiences in those first key years, and end with tips for a successful transition. A few of the people you will meet include…

- Jessica Olsen, who graduated from the Georgia Institute of Technology with a degree in chemical engineering. Within the first five years of her career, she held one patent and had two others pending. She will share how she expanded her impact across the organization.

- Nick Oji, with extensive experience in higher education, will share what he learned transitioning among multiple roles within his career sector.

- Stratton Leopold will share how he balances being a successful, highly regarded movie producer while also managing to run his family's generational ice cream shop in his hometown.

- Alex Crocker, who moved from an individual contributor to a leader in the logistics industry, will share her journey.

- Army Lt. Col (ret) Bill Golden made definite changes in his leadership style, after moving from commanding an elite U.S. Army Special Operations combat helicopter battalion to a New York City global managing director position with a major national bank. He will share his key insights.

- Lisa Shumate, who started her career as a TV anchor and moved into leadership roles in the for-profit commercial world, before shifting to the nonprofit sector in public broadcasting, will share what she learned with every move.

- Tyler Merritt, who transitioned from being a military helicopter pilot to creating a successful clothing line, Nine Line Apparel, will share his biggest new business challenges.

- Mike Siegal, who transitioned from a healthcare executive, to consultant, and then to a rewarding retirement where he applied his skills through volunteerism with Senior Core Of Retired Executives (SCORE), will share his experiences.

That Would Have Been Nice To Know! serves as a guide throughout your career journey. It begins with the transition from your educational experience, and then continues throughout your career, even on into retirement.

Chapter 1 provides insight into the first step in the journey by analyzing the process of moving from formal education to the professional setting. Chapter 2 highlights the opportunities and challenges of moving from one role to another in the same organization. In Chapter 3, you will learn from the transformational experience of leaders who moved from being a frontline employee to a first-time leader. In an environment of constant change, some people find themselves changing career fields altogether. Chapter 4 addresses the mental shifts needed to switch employment arenas entirely. Chapter 5 discusses the challenges and successes of transitioning between for-profit and nonprofit sectors, and Chapter 6 considers the move from military service to civilian life. The transition from the corporate world to becoming an entrepreneur is addressed in Chapter 7. And finally, many people prepare financially for retirement; however, there is still much more to consider. Chapter 8 shares insights from people who have developed their personal retirement plan and discovered how to thrive.

I am pleased you have selected this book to help you through whatever career transition you may be considering or are currently experiencing. Throughout the interviews, consistent patterns of behaviors emerge and are shared in each chapter. The main overriding theme to success was a proactive approach to gaining a greater understanding of oneself and the needs of the organization. The information in this book was gathered through multiple interviews, research, and my personal leadership and work transition experience, with the desire to help you make your transition successfully. By applying the concepts shared in each chapter, you will enhance your chances of thriving in any new career role you pursue.

As a special gift for those who have purchased this book, I have a section on my website with additional free resources that can be easily accessed at www.workplaceadvancement.com/bookclub, password nicetoknow.

Chapter 1
LET'S GET STARTED

You are not your resume, you are your work.

Seth Godin

Many recently hired graduates find themselves excited yet unsure as they transition into their new role in the career world. The excitement for a new stage in life often turns into a big dose of reality that might not match prior expectations. A recognition of the new work world reality and how it is addressed can have a long-term impact on your career trajectory and your success. This chapter will share tips and advice from interviews with people who have successfully made the transition to their new roles. Their insights (and often humorous stories) regarding their new job experiences that were good, and those that could have been better, as well as their advice to new graduates, are designed to assist others who may be embarking on the pathway to a new career.

First, meet Ali Hobbs who graduated from Clemson University with a master's degree in industrial engineering. As she prepared for her first role as a healthcare consultant with Catalyst, a Haskell company, she reviewed books and resources from school and decided which ones she would need in her new role. She analyzed materials, emails, and other resources to be as prepared as possible to begin her first job. She laughs as she shares this story. "If I wasn't successful, it wasn't going to be because I wasn't prepared. I thought I had it all together."

Then, as she started her new role, she learned that she would not need *any* of the material she brought with her, and she knew not nearly enough about her new industry. She realized she was not as prepared as she thought—she actually had perhaps only 10–20 percent of the knowledge she needed to be successful. It was quite humbling, she remembered.

In another scenario, after playing football for Georgia Southern University and graduating with a degree in sports medicine, Nardo Govan began trying to find the right role to match his desire to determine his own hours and pay opportunities. He decided to start his career by joining the International Longshoreman Association to begin work at the Georgia Ports in Savannah, Georgia.

He too discovered the importance of learning the organization and changing his mindset. He realized right from the start that he needed to sell himself and his work ethic, while also analyzing his new environment and culture. When he was a freshman in college, everyone knew he was a freshman, but he did not understand why. Then, he started paying attention to his classmates and realized they all were still acting as if they were in high school. As he began work at the Georgia Ports, he noticed people watching his behavior to determine if he had matured past his college actions and attitudes, and if he had adopted a work world mindset. He realized in those early days that his actions were building his personal "brand," which would follow him throughout his career.

Transitioning from a college mindset to a career mindset needs to be intentional. As a chemical engineering graduate from Georgia Tech, Jessica Olsen worked as a co-op student with Sealed Air Corporation. She would complete a semester at Georgia Tech, then work for Sealed Air for a semester. Her total experience with Sealed Air equated to three school semesters or one and one-half years of work experience.

The co-op experience provided Jessica with a foundation of industrial and organizational knowledge, which made the transition to the career world a bit easier.

Upon graduation, the company offered Jessica a job, but even after joining the organization where she had those semesters of experience as a student, the transition was still a challenge. One of the first hurdles was changing the perceptions of others and helping them see her as a professional rather than as a student. The co-op experience helped Jessica learn the technical aspects of the role, introduced her to the organization, and taught her business acumen. However, her experience was as a student, and she knew some coworkers still perceived her as such. Starting with this knowledge, she soon realized that she had to change some of her behaviors to help others see her in her new role as a professional.

Creating a Personal Brand

All three of these new entrants into the career world realized their actions and attitudes in the first few months on the job were extremely important. Nardo had learned during his university years the importance of building a personal brand and consciously decided what he wanted to be known for, and matched his behavior with, his desired "brand." He was very intentional in his work behaviors. To ensure he was on his best game at work, each day when he arrived at work and before he left his car, he would take a minute to make sure that he had the right work mindset.

As Nardo entered the workplace, he would be cordial and greet people professionally in the office; however, he was cautious about building strong personal relationships in the beginning. It was important for him to be nice to everyone, build a network, assess himself, and most importantly, do the job! These actions begin to build credibility based on a foundation of respect. It is not enough to simply show up and do your job. You need to show that you are needed. It is about proving your value, and that requires self-awareness and being your best all the time. He never knew who might walk into the office, so he needed to be professional at all times. If someone sees you goofing off while work needs to be done, it damages your brand and your image, and it takes a lot more to restore your reputation once it has been questioned.

To build your brand, start with where you want to go and what you want to be known for in the organization. Nardo spent time before graduating from Georgia Southern determining his brand. He identified his work ethic, how he wanted to be perceived by others, and the behaviors that supported his personal brand to ensure that in the first few months on the job, he would make a good impression.

For Jessica, it started with an intention statement. An intention statement defines who you want to be, how you want to contribute, and how you will touch the lives of others. As you create your personal brand, consider what you want others saying about you and how you can support your message through your behavior. For example, if you want to be known as a trustworthy person, demonstrate behaviors that build trust, such as consistently arriving on time, fulfilling commitments, communicating honestly, admitting mistakes, and trusting others. Trust is about credibility. Identify how you can build your credibility. Determine behaviors that might not align with your desired brand and eliminate them.

It is not about being perfect, but it is important to behave intentionally and deliver in the best way possible. People recognize that everyone makes mistakes, but if you have built respect and a good reputation, when you have a bad day, people already know your work ethic and are willing to understand that whatever happened, however unfortunate, was simply a mistake.

Corporate Communications Aren't the Same as College Communications

As you start with a company or organization, regardless of your preparation, you will have much to learn. One area of focus should be on communicating for success. Communication in the business arena is different from communicating with professors or peers. Depending on the role, the level of detail is often different.

At first, Jessica found herself oversharing every nitty-gritty detail of a project with her manager. If a trial went wrong, she would immediately inform her manager that this certain step in the process didn't work, neglecting to share that ten other options existed. In reality, the manager wanted to know the project status and the impact to the bottom line. Was the project progressing as scheduled? Will it meet deadlines? Will the outcome be as expected? The manager did not need to know every step in the process, and he really only needed and wanted to hear about project progression and time estimate to completion.

This was different from Jessica's experience in the academic arena. In school, she was expected to share details, her findings, and everything she did to reach her result. In business, her communications were expected to be results-oriented and focused on the bottom line.

Ali found business communications were different from her usual past communication style as well. After her emails were not getting the results she anticipated, she realized that even though she had written tons of emails in college, she did not know how to write an effective business email. Her emails were too nice and very wordy.

In an attempt to be polite and not sound too aggressive, Ali's emails were not clear, as concise as needed, or assertive. When it came to asking for information, she would end the request with "If you could send it to me by perhaps Friday, that would be nice." The emails were beating around the bush, playing innocent, and trying not to step on anyone's toes. She didn't want to be seen as bossy. However, she actually was reinforcing the perception that she was the new graduate, and it did not convey the professional image she desired.

Every organization has basic business written and verbal presentation norms. Taking the time to learn your organization, the culture of communication, and your manager's style will help you adapt your communication style to your manager and your organization and ultimately lead to greater success. As you transition to the career world, there are many ways to build strong business communication skills. Here are a few ideas to consider:

- Communications you received from the organization before you started with the company will help you understand more about the style of the organization.
- Pay attention to the culture.
- Listen to how people communicate in meetings.
- Watch how leaders communicate.
- Pay special attention to the communication style of those who are successful in the organization.

If needed, consider taking a business communication class. However you proceed, make an intentional plan to enhance your communication style and skill (written and verbal) to match the culture of your organization and your industry.

Back to School

The need to learn more about the organization and the industry was a common surprise and rookie mistake. As the newest and often the youngest members of the team, Jessica, Nardo, and Ali realized quickly that they had a lot to learn. That meant dropping the idea that the degree prepared them totally for their new role and then working to fill their knowledge gaps.

Jessica started by writing out her goals for the next year, three years, and five years, and what she needed to do to reach those goals. Although it may seem easy to assume the organization will provide the information needed and guide you on your career path, Jessica, Nardo, and Ali each shared that they needed to take responsibility for their own learning and growth. They had to be assertive, yet respectful, and ask for the development support they needed if they wanted to expand their level of contribution to the organization.

To build skills, it is important to be critically self-aware and honest with yourself. Do an inventory of your current skill set and the new skills it will take to advance. Be open to multiple learning avenues even those that may not appear so obvious.

Start with understanding what you can contribute to the organization now. Determine what skills you possess that will help the organization move forward. Be cautious about how you address tasks or assignments that might seem beneath you. Although these may be perceived as entry-level tasks or outside of your assigned "lane," it is an opportunity to contribute, excel, impress others, and begin to build your professional brand and portfolio.

Then, exceed expectations with each assignment. Ask what else you can do. After completing each assignment, reflect on what you learned from it. How might this assignment contribute to your brand? How could it have been done better or differently? Learn the "why" behind the assignments and show an interest in the organization by asking questions. Every task or assignment that is done relates to the organization's product, service, and ultimately the bottom line. If you want to add value, you must understand how you are helping improve the all-important bottom line.

Next, consider the new skills you will need to advance and how you can learn them. Do you need to enroll in a formal course? Could you learn these skills from a mentor? Is there a job assignment that may help you to gain these skills? Do you need to consider multiple strategies to build your expertise?

Ali realized she needed to better understand hospital finance, so she enrolled in and completed an online healthcare course. Jessica decided she wanted to be a project manager and understood it was up to her to do what was necessary to make that happen. In her case, she found a mentor who helped her better understand the role and skills needed and specifically how that role worked within her organization. She also took classes to prepare for the Project Management Professional (PMP) Certification, and once she completed the certification, with the mentoring and personal commitment to self-development, she was promoted from her technical role to a project management position.

How will you obtain new skills? What resources are available to continue your learning journey? It is up to you, so be proactive, develop your plan, and then pursue it.

Learning from Many Mentors

As Jessica experienced, learning from mentors is a great way to gain organizational and technical knowledge quickly. Some organizations proactively assign mentors to new employees upon joining the organization. Others may provide mentors once you have established yourself with the organization. However, some organizations do not have a formal mentoring program.

Luckily, there is nothing that says you cannot seek out mentors yourself! Be intentional about identifying a mentor. To be proactive, some employees will simply ask a leader in the organization to be their mentor. It sounds like the right thing to do, but if you don't know what you want to learn, it is hard for the mentor to help and even less likely they will be willing to invest their invaluable time and expertise in you.

Before asking someone to be your mentor, do your homework.

Again, look at the gaps in your knowledge and expertise and then seek out people you know or who have a reputation of being good at what you want to learn. Ali needed mentoring regarding writing effective business emails. She found someone who was good at that and asked for help. In addition to assisting her with emails, she helped Ali better understand the corporate culture and professional behaviors and even became a trusted confidant.

Jessica identified several areas and looked for multiple mentors. She identified someone who could provide her with the scientific and technical knowledge she needed, someone else who could help her learn the organization, and yet another person for professional mentoring. Specifically, she identified someone who was good with building relationships, someone who was good with the equipment, and peers who may have experienced some of the same challenges she was facing, both technically and professionally.

With the right planning, finding a mentor does not have to be difficult. It starts with knowing what you want.

- Do you want to learn more about the culture?
- Do you need to gain technical expertise?
- Do you need someone who can introduce or connect you with others in the organization or industry?

The more specific you can be with your request, the more likely others may be willing to help. Once you identify what you need, brainstorm who you know inside and outside of the organization who may be able to help. In addition to people in the organization, consider family members, neighbors, business contacts, and peers in the industry. Review the total list and determine who may be able to connect you with others, provide advice, teach you a new skill, or sponsor you in the organization. Be prepared to share with each of them what you need and how they can help. Do not stop with one mentor. One person can rarely provide mentoring across different categories.

And finally, understand the relationship should be reciprocal. Be appreciative of those who give of their time and talents to help you succeed, and identify ways you can give back, generally through visible improvements in your work effort, productivity, and advancement. In addition to giving back to your mentor, consider ways to contribute to your organization, your community, and others.

Relationships

Your mom probably warned you about the importance of being careful with whom you associate. It was good advice when you were growing up, and it is still important as you move into your career. You hear the importance of building strong relationships at work but be mindful of the nature of the relationships and the possible perceptions of others.

Jessica, being a rather focused and serious engineer, was walking to check on a product trial with a peer. As they made their way to the lab, her peer began skipping and running down the hallway. Several people were on their way to meetings and noticed this behavior. When Jessica returned to her workspace, her manager asked what she was doing earlier. Surprised, Jessica asked what he was talking about. He responded, "I heard you were having some fun." He assumed she was skipping down the hall and goofing off along with the co-worker. She immediately clarified that she was not goofing off, and luckily, her manager knew her well enough to know the reported feedback was inconsistent with Jessica's work style. Another manager advised her to be careful of her associations and to pay attention to coworkers around her who may try to do as little as possible while getting by on the coattails of others.

Ali shared the same advice and referred to those who behaved in this manner as "picky eaters." That reference is to a child who doesn't want to eat vegetables, so they push them around the plate, spreading them out, and hoping to make it look as if they have been eaten. In a team, the "picky eater" is the employee who pushes his work around, talks about the work, but never actually completes the task at hand.

Although this behavior may appear to work in the short run, it is ultimately discovered and addressed, generally without a positive outcome. Be careful, then, not to be a "picky eater," and do not hang out with those who are. Unfortunately, the people with whom you associate, if you are not aware and cautious, can negatively impact your professional reputation and ultimately limit your career opportunities.

Conversely, by avoiding "picky eaters" and focusing on building strong relationships throughout the organization with those who are serious about personal productivity, more benefits will likely follow. Nardo approached relationship-building by taking the time to observe the relationship dynamics within the team, while being genuine and courteous to everyone.

Building trusting relationships over time builds a network of support that is quite beneficial when you need help. Additionally, it can improve teamwork, which benefits the employer through greater productivity, and strengthens employee morale. Good relationships also provide the opportunity to brainstorm options with peers regarding challenges that you may not want to take to your manager. However, do not let your relationship-building in the form of brainstorming and having fun slip into venting and become unprofessional.

At one organization, new college graduates were put in a section of the building that was full of cubicles. The new staff members then began to refer to their space as the "Cube Farm," which was rarely visited by leadership. In the spirit of being friendly, some staff would fly paper airplanes in the office along with other behaviors that might have been acceptable in college but not in a regular office environment. They thought it was fun and simply lightened the mood from time to time until one day, you guessed it, a leader walked by and observed this unprofessional behavior. They quickly learned a very hard lesson of how inappropriate behavior can limit their opportunities and impact their personal brand.

New graduates often wonder if they should develop strong personal relationships at work. This is a tough question. The answer depends on many factors, including the organizational culture and the nature of the relationship. Overall, be very cautious. Even if you think you are keeping your personal and professional life separate, any observed misstep can result in embarrassing consequences.

In one instance, Ali was repeatedly asked out by a coworker. She was new to the organization and did not want to start a socially personal relationship with someone in the same office. She politely declined his invitations. However, the requests for dates continued, and she continued to say no.

Frustrated and in haste, Ali texted two of her friends to say she had finally told him "absolutely not" and added some extraneous girl talk. However, her work contacts and her personal contacts were merged on her phone. She had accidentally sent the full text message to her director! It seems she had his cell number on her phone, although she had never used it since he was much higher in the organization, and, to that point, she had very few interactions with him.

Realizing her mistake, she panicked and immediately went to the information technology department (IT) to try to get the text message retracted. But of course, it could not be done. So…not only did the director know of her at work "girl issue," but others in her own department and IT knew as well! Be careful to avoid intermingling your personal and professional information.

Building professional relationships in an organization does not have to be difficult. There are many successful ways to incorporate these in your daily routines.

- If you habitually eat lunch at your desk, stop! Get away from your desk or cubicle and eat with other people. You may be pleasantly surprised by the connections that can be built over casual lunch conversations.
- Participate in organizational networking events, corporate-sponsored community events, and volunteer opportunities.
- Attend lunch and learns and speak to others at the session. Show an interest in peers who are participating in projects by asking questions about their work.

Jessica found that asking questions about a project, even those seemingly small and unimportant, opened doors to new connections throughout the organization. At times, her question might require expertise from someone who was not directly linked to the project. By requesting help from an expert elsewhere in the company, she added to her employee network.

Ask for Help!

Asking questions and asking for help is not only a good idea, but it is often expected by supervisors. Employees who do not ask for help are the ones who can actually scare managers the most! Managers and peers may have been doing the job for so long that procedures that seem obvious to them are not so obvious to someone new.

Your first questions, certainly as a new employee, should be related to supervisory expectations, both of you personally and for your role, understanding it often takes 12– 24 months to feel comfortable in a new role. Do not assume you know what the manager is expecting. Ask specifically about your responsibilities, the amount of decision-making you can exercise, outcomes expected, deadlines, and important people you should know inside and outside of the team.

As you begin working on projects, elements of the job that you do not know or expect will emerge. Understand that no one knows everything, and collective minds create better outcomes. Ask for the help and support you need, and when appropriate, use your lack of information to your advantage. Acknowledge upfront that this is new and you have a few questions. Some of the questions you ask may prompt your peers to look at the project from a fresh perspective.

A word of caution when asking questions. Timing and setting are important. If the question is technical, it may need to be asked in a technical setting, as opposed to a more general business meeting. Otherwise, your technical question may unnecessarily derail the meeting.

If the question is related to common knowledge in the industry, you may be able to get your question answered by doing your own research. Also, recognize the intent of your question. Are you asking the question to increase knowledge or because you do not agree? At times, others in the organization may have more knowledge on an issue and may make a decision you do not agree with or understand. Recognize when it is time to quit asking, accept the decision, and move ahead with your assigned work.

On a Personal Note

When someone progresses on their journey from college to career, they are also becoming more independent. With the increased independence, two additional topics are important to cover in this chapter: personal finance and safety. If these are not handled properly, it can create stress, which can impact productivity, morale, and personal satisfaction.

Nardo shared his biggest surprise in his new role was the random and unexpected bills in his personal life. He planned for his known bills and believed he would have enough money to cover everything but soon learned he had unexpected bills, such as insurance, car maintenance, and taxes, to name a few. He realized that just because he had money, he did not need to spend it all. He strongly advises building a savings account, and then, of course, spending money wisely. That is not to say you should never go out with friends, but just stay aware of how much you are spending and balance that social spending with a focus on saving for the future.

Personal safety is of the upmost importance, especially in today's complex society. You may be starting your career in a new location or a new city. You may be required to travel for work, or you may be living alone for the first time. You should be aware of your surroundings and have at least a basic understanding of self-defense techniques.

Jessica took a Krav Maga class in college and later became an instructor. In addition to providing a foundation for self-defense techniques, it provided her with a way to stay fit and meet new people. Research several self-defense offerings which may include C.O.B.R.A, Krav Maga, and other martial arts programs. Check out your local self-defense courses offered by organizations in the community, the police department, or online. Please take your safety seriously!

Recommended Action Steps from Those Who Went Before You

Preparing for success in your new role requires initiative and a willingness to take personal responsibility for your development. Here are some tips on how to make the transition to the world of work more effectively.

Create a personal brand. It is OK to recognize that you cannot be perfect at everything. Understand your strengths and how they can be beneficial to the organization. Be honest with yourself, take personality inventories and self-assessment quizzes, and ask for feedback, with the intent to gain a better understanding of yourself and assignments and roles that may leverage your strengths.

Understand the organization's communication style. Review the information you received from the organization and notice the communication style. Pay attention to the culture, the discussion in meetings, how leaders communicate, and especially the communication style of those who are successful in the organization. Make a plan to match your communication style to the organizational culture.

Know the industry. Join industry email threads. Most industries have organizations that provide updated information on their specific sector. Research articles, journals, blogs, and other organizations that provide updates and trends. Some information may be daily; other information may be posted routinely but less frequently. It is a great way to stay informed while growing your knowledge base.

Educate yourself. In addition to joining industry emails and posting sites, look for additional methods of growing your expertise. Ali moved into the healthcare industry and had limited information. One step she took was to review the curriculum for a master's program in healthcare administration, to determine what she knew and what was different. Needing to learn more about healthcare reimbursement specifically, Ali signed up for an online course on healthcare finance through Coursera. Take full advantage of the vast quantity of information sources out there and available to you.

Learn from many mentors. Get a mentor or several mentors! Find people inside and outside the organization who have the expertise you need and ask for help. Solicit several mentors with diverse skills and build a network for development and support. Be grateful and reciprocate.

Build strong relationships at every level in the organization. Collaboration is imperative for your success and building relationships throughout the organization can dramatically impact your progress and reduce your stress levels. Consider your relationships as collaborations that are reciprocal. Think not only about how they can help you, but how you can best help them. Invest in helping others and they will be there to help you when needed. Get to know people with different skill sets and who have a solid reputation within the workplace.

Ask for help! Recognize when you need help, and do not be afraid to ask when needed. It can build relationships and show a willingness to learn. However, when asking for help, be sensitive to the timing and the environment before you ask.

On a personal note: Consider personal factors and living conditions that may change and develop a plan. Create a budget, take a self-defense class, and get active in your community.

You can download your free Brand Building Worksheet at www. workplaceadvancement.com/bookclub, password nicetoknow.

Chapter 2
SHOULD I CHANGE JOBS IN MY SAME INDUSTRY?

On average, people change jobs every 4.2 years.

Bureau of Labor Statistics. Tenure.
September 2020.

If you are happy in your job and you love it, should you consider a new role? Should the new role be in your industry or an entirely new one? Some people are quite happy in their current role, and the thought of change creates angst. However, there are many reasons people consider leaving their current role, and often, although change can be quite stressful, it can be beneficial to your personal growth and career trajectory.

One sign that it may be time for a change is if you know your job so well that you have shifted to "autopilot." When you start to "coast," you can lose your competitive edge and become complacent. Complacency can impact your reputation and put you at risk of falling behind and losing the connection to the industry or recognizing changing trends. Although you may not notice it, it's almost certain that others will.

Changing jobs can keep you more engaged, widen your experience, broaden your knowledge base, increase your earning power, and make you more valuable to the organization. The focus of this chapter will be making career moves within the same industry with experts from technology, education, and higher education sharing their experiences and advice. Although you may not be in one of these fields, the concepts can be transferred to most any career move.

Let's start with technology. Though he was born in the United States, Andy Cabistan grew up in Costa Rica. He knew he wanted to work in the tech industry at a very early age. At the age of 16, at his insistence, his parents put him on a plane with a one-way ticket bound for the United States. That would be scary to most people, but Andy was excited and knew that was his ticket to accomplishing his dream.

Andy committed himself to learning and pursuing his passion to work in the technology field. Originally, Andy thought he would have to be a software engineer to get a job in technology; however, he soon learned of many tech jobs, including marketing, sales, and customer service. After graduating from Armstrong State University (now Georgia Southern University), Andy started his own company to develop a tech platform using psychometric tools to enhance communication. This experience provided him with fundamental business acumen. However, he wanted to move to a larger corporate role in technology.

After two years, Andy closed his business and joined an organization as a sales development representative responsible for generating business opportunities, which he really enjoyed. It confirmed his passion for the tech industry and eventually led him to move to the mecca of tech in Silicon Valley. He accepted a position as a sales development representative for a tech start-up in San Francisco, ultimately landing a position as an account executive at a fast-growing startup organization.

Most of Andy's moves were lateral, with no new prestige or additional money. However, when asked if they were beneficial moves, Andy responded with an unequivocal, "Yes!" Andy is ambitious and felt each lateral move taught him new skills and ultimately opened future opportunities and expanded his network.

As an elementary school teacher in the public school system, Lauren Olsen taught different grade levels every year for the first four years of teaching. She found that learning the expectations in different grade levels helped her to understand the learning progression and how her role in each grade fit within the broader student progression. After enjoying four years of teaching in a Title One school environment, Lauren pursued an opportunity to move to a new elementary school.

It was the school she attended as a child, and, in fact, the very school where she decided early on to become a teacher. To make the potential move even more attractive, the position would be teaching second grade in the classroom right next to the original second-grade teacher who inspired her to make elementary education her career. Lauren's experience in a different school environment, and with multiple grade levels, was attractive to the hiring principal, and Lauren got the job! She accepted the position in the middle of a pandemic, so not only did she move to a new school, everything about teaching was changing as well.

Working in higher education, Nick Oji echoed Andy's sentiments that moving within your industry can be beneficial to your career advancement. Nick worked for a university as the assistant director of student involvement responsible for assessing the student experience, orientation, and community involvement. After about two years in that role, he was asked to consider the role of assistant director of card services. Although he felt prepared for his first role, this new opportunity would require an entirely new skill set, which seemed quite scary to Nick.

He accepted the position and demonstrated the ability to adapt and be successful in a new environment. Then, almost two years later, yet another opportunity outside of his expertise became available, and Nick was asked to move into a faculty recruiter role. Although the role of faculty recruiter wasn't on Nick's carefully thought-out career path, he realized his two previous positions taught him valuable skills that made him uniquely prepared for the challenge.

Many elements should be considered before jumping into a lateral move or a different role. Here are a few to consider:

- First, take an inventory of your transferrable skills. What are the skills needed for the new role, and what skills do you have that will help you be successful?
- Next, consider how willing you are to get out of your safe zone. Staying in the safe zone may be comfortable, but rarely does someone grow when they play it safe.
- Ask questions. Find out about the expectations and skills needed for the new role. Analyze your willingness to become a student again and whether you are willing to put in the effort needed to learn new skills.
- Finally, take calculated risks. Not every role is worth the risk, but don't allow yourself to become too cautious either.

Andy, Lauren, and Nick all took calculated risks and believe the moves they embraced prepared them for their later new roles. Andy learned how to run a business and how sales fit in the overall organizational plan. Lauren learned how each grade level fits into the overall education path and how to work with students from all backgrounds. Nick's first role required heavy emphasis on people skills while his second role relied heavily on technical expertise. His third one required a combination of these skill sets; therefore, the lateral moves contributed heavily to his success. Here is their advice for a successful transition.

Strategies for the First 90 Days

As with any role, your first few months on the job will impact your reputation and long-term success, so a well thought out plan is needed. To start your role with clarity, meet with your manager to obtain the overall strategic value of the role and the expectations for you. Create a plan for what you hope to accomplish in the first 30, 60, and 90 days. Consider your transferable skills and how you can add value immediately. Ask your manager for his or her expectations of you in the same 30-, 60-, and 90-day timeframes. Compare the two perspectives and create an agreed-upon plan with goals that align with the overall organizational strategy and expectations.

Begin building relationships immediately. When Andy starts a new role, he asks for a list of people throughout the organization whom he should meet. On that list, he looks for people in his department whom he will need to work with on projects and people who are the best at a particular skill, such as conducting product demonstrations or understanding the politics of the organization. He also seeks out top performers across departments and leaders from multiple disciplines. He proactively sets up meetings with the people on his list and conducts informational interviews.

According to Andy, "This is a strategy that has been most helpful for gaining organizational knowledge and building relationships." Then, he takes it a step further. When a new leader joins the organization, he sends a welcome email and a request for a meeting. This simple act builds goodwill and enhances collaboration, which ultimately benefits the customer. When a customer has a request or recommendation, Andy knows the system, has built relationships, and can send the feedback to the right person, allowing him to provide better customer service.

Lauren learned it was important to gain trust with her new coworkers quickly. She knew she needed to determine how she was going to fit into the culture and the dynamics at both her new school and grade level. Luckily, she would be working with her original second-grade teacher and mentor, which made it comfortable for her to seek answers to her questions and address any concerns.

Lauren realized she would be the youngest on the second-grade team, with the other teachers being experienced, not only in their profession, but at the school. They had been working together and had already built strong relationships. Since she was starting her new role in the middle of a pandemic and teachers were moving to a virtual teaching environment, Lauren was able to bring fresh ideas and much needed technical assistance to her colleagues. Her coworkers responded in-kind and assisted her with second-grade resources and acclimated her to new student and parent expectations.

Another important element to consider in the first 90 days is understanding the culture and expectations. Lauren moved from a team where teachers discussed curriculum, but where each teacher developed his or her own strategies, to a school where grade level teamwork was the norm. Understanding the accepted norms helped greatly with Lauren's rapid adaptation and transition to a new school.

Although Lauren had been successful with both her school's administration and students in the past, her new school brought different expectations from students, parents, and the administration, which required additional changes to her teaching and relationship style. Being assertive and asking questions regarding the expectations and culture helped Lauren to adapt more quickly and effectively.

When starting a new role, be curious. Gaining an understanding of the environment in which you work can help you contribute sooner and more productively. Take time to assess the current situation and observe others who are strong performers to determine what they do that has led them to be successful. Ask questions to gain a better overall perspective of the team and organizational culture, expectations, reputation, and strengths and how the organization competes in the industry. Find out the team's role in the organization's success and what processes or resources are available to you.

Be Helpful!

Building relationships is invaluable; however, don't make the mistake of making the relationship only about what you can get, while not considering what you can give. Nick is naturally drawn to people and has an innate desire to help. Not only is relationship-building natural to him, but he sees the value of investing in relationships early, even those that he doesn't think will help him.

If Nick can help, he is happy to do it, and in addition to the instant gratification, he considers it an investment in that person's "emotional bank account." He also knows the day will come when he has an unexpected need and will have to make a "withdrawal" from one of his coworkers' "emotional bank accounts." He wants to ensure, through his continued helping of colleagues, that there is something in the bank to withdraw! He stated, "If there are no investments in the emotional bank account, the withdrawal may come with a hefty 'fine,' meaning you may find yourself with expected, yet difficult favors, or even worse, poor relationships." Coworkers whom you have helped typically will be glad to help when you are in need. Your behavior each day determines your relationships. The coworkers who have had poor experiences with you, or perhaps feel as if you are internally focused and not willing to help others, are exactly the ones who will charge the largest "fine," or not help at all. Helping colleagues when needed is critical. Even if you see no future payoff, invest in building quality relationships with your peers and with others throughout the organization.

Andy learned early to build reciprocal relationships and has the motto "sharing is caring." As he started a new role in sales, he realized he could create tools that led to greater productivity and that could be helpful to others. It became his forte, and he shared his tools, knowledge, and new processes regarding generating leads with other sales representatives in his new organization. Although sharing this type of information was not the norm in his industry, he knew it was the right thing to do and it paid off.

Once Andy shared, others were willing to share. He found the skills he lacked could be learned from more experienced members of the team. By offering his expertise and assistance, others were willing to share their expertise, and that helped Andy accomplish his development goals of gaining better negotiating tactics and improving his executive presence.

As you start a new position, consider how you can help your team members and others in the organization. What are the specific skills you have that can improve the productivity of the team, build relationships, or enhance teamwork? Carefully assess the environment to determine the best way to offer your ideas and to be helpful. If your assistance is not offered in the context of the culture, there is a risk of being perceived as an "obnoxious know it all" who doesn't understand the organization. When trying to build a new career, no one wants that reputation.

Learning Comes in a Variety of Formats

As a child, your learning curve is very steep, and you are expected to continue to grow and expand your knowledge each year, especially in school. As an adult, some believe it is time to simply put the learning into practice, but if you stop learning, you will fall behind in your job and your industry. Learning comes in many formats. Many decide to continue their development through formal channels of education, while others grow through informal learning, and others through experiential learning. Often, it is a combination of these.

Formal education is widely available at technical schools, universities, and online. To excel in her teaching career, Lauren decided to pursue additional formal education by enrolling in a master's degree program in education to broaden her exposure to different perspectives in the teaching profession. Andy enrolled in an online boot camp focused on sales development representatives, which ultimately opened doors to his dream job and his desired destination in Silicon Valley.

Nick learned simply by asking for input from his team and others in his network and the industry. Be certain not to overlook those obvious resources close at hand.

An informal method of growing and broadening your skills is through networking. Most people think of networking as a way to land a new role or develop business leads. Although certainly true, networking can also build your expertise and confidence and help you stay up to date on industry trends.

Andy uses networking to increase his industry knowledge. He looks for people who may be in similar roles in different companies and asks for a meeting, virtually or in person. Recently, he researched and found someone at Amazon who had dealings in the same business sector. He sent a brief email letting her know he worked with similar clients and would like to discuss some of the specific nuances in their business. In less than 24 hours, he received a response, and a meeting was set up. it turned out to be quite insightful, and now he has a new contact in his growing network.

Although meaning well, Nick learned a tough lesson regarding the necessity of learning and listening to others from a situation that did not work out as well for him. In a previous role as a DJ, Nick had the opportunity to meet many Grammy Award winners. When his organization was organizing a fundraiser, he eagerly offered to help. He secured a few artists to perform and made all the arrangements for the event. He was sure he knew what he was doing, so when others mentioned that the numbers did not add up, he dismissed their concerns, knowing they had no experience in the music industry.

Nick moved forward with his unchanged plan. As it turned out, Nick missed several factors in the budget and the event barely broke even. After a few days of feeling extremely down, defeated, and embarrassed, Nick decided to figure out what he could learn from the experience and realized he had undervalued the opinions of others who had expertise they were willing to share. It was a difficult experience but a great lesson. Now he is open to the opinions of others and proactively seeks their input.

Lauren also shared the importance of learning by listening to others and the impact on her personally. As she transferred to a new school environment, she recalled thinking, "I know I'm a good teacher, and I know the worth that I bring to the classroom." However, she also realized that not everyone would appreciate her style, so it would be important to listen to the teachers who had been there for years that the parents already loved. It was those teachers who had a lot of wisdom to share and were especially helpful with improving her parent communications. She stated, "If I had not listened to them and I had rested on my thoughts that, 'I am a good teacher, I know how to speak to parents, I'll be fine,' I would not be as successful as I currently am with my parents. Turns out, these parent expectations are quite different from the previous ones I worked with."

Assess the Environment

Every organization has a different culture, and Lauren discovered understanding the environment in which you work and its daily norms are vitally important. Although it would be easy to think teaching in an elementary school would be the same regardless of the school, Lauren found that not to be true. The number of administrative classroom observations varied, as did the expectations of what should be accomplished during planning periods. Teacher interactions and the norms regarding teamwork and lesson planning also varied. Lauren advises people starting in a new role not to simply continue in their previous patterns of behavior, but to identify which ones are valued in their new location and adapt quickly. What made you successful in one role may not be the behaviors that will make you successful in your new one.

Although Nick was moving from one leadership role to another in the same university, he described his first step as, "...coming alongside the team and understanding the problems they face, and then understanding the different roles on the team and how to facilitate everyone working together to accomplish their goals." He spent the first six months in his new role building relationships and learning. Specifically, he asked questions regarding what each person did, what they were good at, what mistakes had been made, (and why), and what they should be doing but weren't yet. He recalled that he felt as if he was back in school. However, Nick was making incremental changes along the way, such as implementing new technology and training, but it wasn't until 12–24 months later that he felt he was getting strong tangible results.

According to Andy, anyone in sales understands that at times they may need to bend the rules to make a customer happy. However, he learned the hard way that before you bend the rules, you need to understand the impact of your decisions and to balance it with how far you can push. He recalled a specific instance where he went directly to a vice president who was several levels above him to try to get something approved. Unfortunately, this action resulted later in a difficult conversation with his manager in the conference room.

In another instance, he was pushing the limits on a specific process and was told by his manager the risk of his actions. His manager stated, "These people you are trying to work around, you still need them. They will be helping you on the two or three steps after what you want to get done right now. Don't make friction at this stage because if you make friction, they may not want to help you next time. Relationships are the key." If Andy had taken the time to better understand the processes, where his role fit into the larger chain, and how the organization worked, he could have saved himself some personal grief and avoided a few mistakes. Again, this experience emphasizes the importance of understanding one's new culture and building relationships.

In the school setting, Lauren found it helpful in relationship building to conduct vertical planning with the teachers one grade higher than where she was teaching and one grade lower. Lauren met with a third-grade teacher to better understand where the student skills should be by the end of third grade. Knowing this helped Lauren better prepare her students and allowed her to push her students past the second-grade standards and have them better prepared for third grade. She offered the same information to the first-grade teachers as well. Taking this approach enhanced teamwork, not only at her grade level, but with the teachers who interact with the students before and after second grade. This effort can ultimately increase students' growth rates from year to year.

Understanding Yourself and Others

Once you understand the culture and organization, you may have to adapt your skills for success in your new role. Take an inventory of your skills and think how they can be adapted to add productive value. Adding value may take time and may require learning new skills, being flexible, or using your skills in a new way.

Nick knew he enjoyed building relationships and inspiring people. That was a natural fit for his first role, where he led the volunteer organizations for students, staff, and faculty. However, in his second role, he was the leader in a technology department that required him to be more task-oriented and to learn operational skills like scheduling, budgeting, goal setting, and mapping out action plans. He had to figure out how to take the big picture and break it into smaller pieces that could be worked on incrementally. And although that role was not on his carefully planned career trajectory, he stated, "It was probably the most amazing learning experience that I've ever had on a job." In his third role at the university, he realized the position required a blend of people skills from the first role and operational skills from his second one. He felt what he learned in the two roles had definitely contributed to his success in his faculty recruitment position. For Nick, it was about understanding how to adapt and apply his previous skills in a new way and being open to learning new skills for the job.

Andy is a very direct person and typically will humorously share his thoughts. However, he recalled one instance when he said something to his manager that he does NOT recommend you do unless you have a very good relationship and a strong understanding of the culture. He was then reporting to a man who was under a lot of stress to meet company goals, and this manager was not handling it well. One week, the manager's behavior was particularly tough, and in a one-on-one meeting between Andy and his manager, the manager asked if he had any comments. Andy hesitated then said, "Yes. I think you are unstable." Then, he realized what he said and could not believe he said that to his hiring manager! Even so, Andy knew the manager was basically a good man, and Andy felt the environment was one where he felt safe sharing his thoughts. Luckily for Andy, the manager agreed his behavior had been out of line, and as a thank you for his honesty, the manager gave Andy a business book he knew Andy had been wanting to read.

Before you consider anything like this, assess the manager, your relationship, and the organization to determine what is safe to say. Andy was fortunate in that instance. He cautions that rarely does being that blunt work out for you!

How you handle setbacks will demonstrate your character. Nick struggles with maintaining perspective. When goals are missed or results are not achieved, he has to fight the tendency to focus on the mistakes and not let the disappointment become magnified. He stated, "I get caught in the quagmire and I see all the bad stuff happening and how I'm not hitting goals or achieving results. Then I start to beat myself up." He learned that keeping his thoughts in perspective and focusing on what is working and the progress being made helps him maintain a better attitude and overcome the challenges faster.

Throughout this chapter, examples of the importance of knowing yourself, your new role, and the new team becomes clear as you make a career transition. Andy, Lauren, and Nick each looked at their skills and strengths and took calculated risks when it came to moves within their employment sector. By maintaining a learning perspective, they were able to adapt their talents and skills to each new environment, which they believe contributed to a successful career transition.

Recommended Action Steps from Those Who Went Before You

Create your plan for what you hope to accomplish in your first 90 days. Ask your manager for their expectations of you and ask questions to be sure you understand how you will be measured. Your plan should include how you will build relationships throughout the organization and how you will gain trust quickly.

Be positive. Not only is it important that you are positive about your current role, but discussions regarding previous roles and teams also need to stay positive. Write down a few actions that can help you stay positive. Will you keep a journal of the good things that make you happy at your place of employment? Will you subscribe to a blog that encourages positivity? Will you focus on the positive aspects of your role during your quiet time? Will you hang out with positive people? Be intentional and specific with your plan.

Be flexible. Your career trajectory may not take you in the direction you outlined, so stay open to new experiences and trying new things. Nick's career did not follow his carefully crafted five-year plan, but by being open and willing to try new areas, he has had great roles that contributed to his professional growth. In the school setting, Lauren accepted a new position at a new school as a second-grade teacher. However, due to enrollment, there was a chance she would need to move to another grade level. Luckily for her, she was able to stay in second grade, but her reputation for being flexible was one of the traits her new principal valued highly. Business needs may dictate shifts in your plan. By being flexible and willing to adapt, you will be successful. If asked to consider a change, take time to think it through carefully before responding.

Be helpful. Consider how your skills can be applied to help your team members and others in the organization. Do you have specific skills that can improve the productivity of the team, build relationships, or enhance teamwork? Carefully assess the environment to determine the best way to offer your ideas and to be helpful.

Learn! Understand your skills as well as the skills you will need to be successful. Where are your skill gaps? Determine the learning resources that are available to you, including peers and specialists in the organization, and create a learning plan that will help you reduce the skills gap.

Network. Although networking may be difficult for you, once it is mastered, the benefits are limitless. If you are uncomfortable with networking, consider an interpersonal communication course or read a book on how to start a conversation. Consider interesting methods to stand out and build relationships at events. Vanessa Van Edwards, in her book *Captivate: The Science of Succeeding with People,* provides valuable insight into how to network and build rapport. Create a monthly plan to improve and expand your network.

Assess the work environment. What is similar and what is different in your new environment? What are the team norms? What is the vocabulary? What are the boundaries? How do departments interact with each other?

Identify how you like to work and the tasks you enjoy. Are you more task-oriented or people-oriented? Do you prefer a fast-paced environment or a slow-paced environment? Would you prefer a structured environment with clear processes, or do you prefer to create new processes? Consider taking a behavioral inventory such as DISC to help discover how you prefer to work. Look for ways to use your natural behavioral style in your new role and determine where you may need to adapt.

Build a strong reputation. Bring your "A" game to work every day. This doesn't mean you have to be perfect. However, strive to be someone who delivers results in a way that builds strong relationships throughout the team and the organization. What can you do that will be memorable to someone at work today? Write it down and do it!

Keep perspective. Don't magnify your mistakes while minimizing your successes. It is easy to become overwhelmed by what you think is a failure without keeping it in perspective. Recognize where you need to improve, but don't lose sight of the positive outcomes and what is working for you. Keep a file or a journal of your successes and visit it frequently to remind you of the positive impact you made!

Learn more about yourself by taking a quick and easy work from home survey that will provide insight into your behavioral preferences and communication accessible at www.workplaceadvancement.com/bookclub, password nicetoknow.

Chapter 3
WHAT THEY DIDN'T TELL YOU ABOUT LEADERSHIP

2,660,000,000

Google

After doing a quick Google search, 2,660,000,000 references were found on leadership, clearly indicating there is an abundance of information on the topic. With so many resources available, why is it so hard to be successful as a leader? Could it be because every individual, every organization, and every leadership experience is different? Yes, absolutely! In addition, there are always things you didn't know going into the role, whether new to the organization, or moving up from within. Several new leaders were willing to share their surprises, as well as the successful strategies they used, as they transitioned into a leadership role for the first time.

Some leaders moved from being a peer to a leader of the same group, while others moved to departments or organizations where they knew few, if any, of those they would lead. Common challenges included:

- Learning the new expectations and perceptions of the role.
- Maneuvering the leadership processes.
- Being responsible for others.
- Learning accountability systems.

Each new leader found success by capitalizing on the skills they had obtained in their earlier roles and learning to apply them in a new way. In addition, being curious and developing a learning mindset were essential. They asked good questions and listened to their team. This chapter shares surprises as well as advice from Ilona Curry, a new human resource information services manager; Alex Crocker, a service center manager; and Stephanie Lamar, a director of preventative health. Although each leader works in a different industry, commonalities in their experiences were discovered.

When Ilona Curry moved from an individual contributor to her leadership role, she was surprised when her self-perception changed. Ilona moved from senior business systems analyst at a small health-care organization to the human resource information systems (HRIS) manager at an international engineering and construction solutions firm within the energy industry. Initially, she started as an independent contributor in the energy division and spent time learning about the industry and the services provided by her new organization.

Power plants, environmental infrastructure, and nuclear plants were all new to her; therefore, she had a lot to learn. At the time, she focused on building her technical expertise as well as industry knowledge. When she was promoted to the HRIS manager, she had new leadership systems and processes to learn, but her biggest surprise was that she felt more confident. When she gained the title of manager, she immediately felt empowered to make decisions and began expressing her thoughts and ideas more assertively.

Alex Crocker, the daughter of an FBI agent, moved around a good bit as a child and therefore was comfortable living in different cities and experiencing new environments. Soon after graduating from Clemson University, she joined a logistics and supply chain services provider as a project lead and then moved into a global account manager position. To gain additional experience in a different industry, she left the organization to work for a consulting firm. She was asked to return to her first company to fill a service center manager role.

When interviewed for this book, Alex's team had about 50 employees with 13 direct reports. In her first role with the company, she worked with many of the same employees she now leads. Her challenge was moving from peer or in some cases, subordinate, to now leading the team. To add to the challenge, Alex was younger than many of her team members. She had to reevaluate the relationships and figure out what mental shifts and actions needed to happen to successfully move from peer and friend to manager.

Stephanie Lamar moved from a social work position in a large hospital system to a director position in the quality department. The position was several levels higher; essentially, she was skipping a few levels along the way. Jumping leadership levels made establishing her credibility important, meaning she had to work through a few first impressions of some of the team members.

Stephanie remembered that when she was introduced to the division as the new director, an experienced volunteer looked at Stephanie and stated, "I'm sorry, I was just expecting someone a little bit older. The last director was older." Stephanie, unphased, shared her age and learned that evidently, she didn't quite look that old. The volunteer immediately replied, "I wish I looked like you when I was that age!" The issue was over and now they work very well together. It was important for Stephanie to address misperceptions honestly and authentically from the start.

As each of these employees moved into their new roles, they needed to learn the new leadership expectations of the organization and change their mindset from frontline contributor to leader. They wrestled with challenges like managing the performance of the team, developing their own leadership style, and creating strategies to motivate the team; however, each was ultimately successful.

The First Few Months

The initial focus of each of the new leaders in their first few months was on learning. They proactively spent time with the team discovering information about the team members, department processes, communication, and outcomes. They sought out leadership training that was provided by the organization and any additional resources that would help address their initial performance gaps. Although each felt somewhat prepared for the role, they still had a lot to learn.

When it came to analyzing and assessing the team, Alex, who was young and had never managed people before, decided to start by conducting one-on-one meetings with each team member. Due to her age and lack of leadership experience, she knew some of the employees questioned her ability to lead, making it imperative that she develop a relationship with each team member, build trust, and establish an open line of communication. The one-on-one meetings provided an avenue for the team members to share their expertise, challenges, and expectations, while learning more about their new manager. At the same time, it provided Alex with the opportunity to build a relationship, gain knowledge of the department, and provide future direction on an individual level.

Stephanie inherited a team that started out small and grew rapidly, so no formal channels of communication had yet been developed between team members. She immediately implemented once-a-week team huddles so that her staff members could touch base, share priorities, and voice challenges. The intent of the huddles was to build a new culture of teamwork, by moving the employees from being workers sharing a location, to a truly cohesive team. She included ice breakers at each huddle so that team members could learn more about each other as well as their respective roles and responsibilities.

Having worked as a team member before becoming the manager of the same unit, Ilona was familiar with the team's expectations, processes, and personalities. With her training and a strong focus on customer service, she was eager to say yes to every leadership request. She did not want to be perceived as a barrier to the organization's success; rather, she wanted to establish herself as a valuable partner to her internal customers. However, she was not ready for the large volume of service requests associated with her new role.

At first, she thought she needed to respond to each request, ensuring each internal customer received exactly what they requested. She quickly learned that she was too eager to please, as some of the requests were not possible or perhaps not in line with the organization's priorities. She had to learn how to tactfully share with people what they actually needed and what they could expect, as opposed to what they thought they wanted, and how to align requests with organizational needs.

These leaders learned how to apply the skills they learned in previous positions to their new leadership role. Alex had been a project manager, requiring her to motivate teams to accomplish goals and to apply tracking systems which were key in her leadership role success. Ilona had a depth of technical expertise but quickly realized it needed to be expanded; therefore, she did additional research and participated in vendor calls to not only do her job better, but also to more effectively assist her team.

Ilona also recalled a critical but fixable mistake she made that had an impact on her leadership style. While building a performance management system, Ilona accidently reversed the computerized rating scale, and she did not realize the mistake until after the system was implemented. Thus, if someone was ranked high by their manager, the system reversed the ranking, making it appear that they were a poor performer. Although she laughs about it now, she learned the importance of planning and she "measures 10 times and cuts once," as the wise carpenter's adage goes. She does her due diligence before making changes and encourages her team to take the time to do the same. It also made her more sympathetic to her team members when they made honest mistakes.

Performance Management

With management comes the responsibility to attract, motivate, and retain employees. Since human resource practices and performance management were new responsibilities for these new leaders, each discovered a steep learning curve. In addition to the need to learn human resource processes, they had to find time to inspire and motivate the team, while also meeting the other responsibilities and expectations of leadership. For a new leader, it is easy to underestimate the amount of time it takes to keep the team fully staffed, engaged, and productive.

Quite often a new leader is provided leadership training. However, at times, it may not include some of the specific steps to complete the HR processes. For Stephanie, that was the case. Luckily, she had a peer who was a seasoned manager and was willing to walk her through the steps of creating a job description, sending the job description for compensation grading, obtaining a job code, and obtaining final supervisory approval—all steps that had to be accomplished before a new position could be posted! These steps were needed to ensure equity between employees throughout the organization and for effective resource utilization, but these processes can be new to someone who has not been in a prior leadership role. If your organization does not provide specific training in this area, seek out help from the human resources department, your mentor, or a seasoned peer.

Alex, who considered herself to be a fairly easy employee to manage, underestimated the time it takes to address people challenges and administrative processes related to management of a team. Initially, she did not factor time for such processes into her schedule and soon discovered the value of having a friend in human resources! At times it took a full day away from her management tasks to address an employee performance issue or to help an employee who was experiencing a personal crisis.

Realizing that addressing these HR concerns was now part of her management responsibility, she made time to learn not only the HR processes, but the reasons behind them. Having not dealt with HR issues previously, she was unaware of the legal implications and the liabilities that were inherent in managing people. As such, she wanted to ensure that she was fair to all employees. Although some of the processes may seem arduous, typically there are valid reasons for each policy or process. Learning more about the "why" behind each policy will help you better understand how to apply them to get the best outcome for your employee and the organization.

Feedback is an important part of managing performance; however, the format and frequency will be quite different based on the department and the organization. In many organizations, performance reviews are held once a year, with the expectation that individual feedback is provided throughout the year. Providing feedback may not be a top priority in some fast-paced organizations, but for Alex, it became a priority.

Best practices suggest feedback should be on-going, formal and informal, and provided with the intent of providing specific information on performance, both when the employee excels, and when the employee needs to improve. Alex strongly believes feedback should be provided in real time and should be compassionately honest. With development as a primary goal, she created a template for performance discussions that was focused on six key categories. Using that template, she then conducted individual quarterly meetings with each team member.

In these meetings, Alex encouraged her employee to share their observed strengths, what they hoped to learn, and how they could improve their performance. After hearing their thoughts, Alex would share her perspective on each employee's strengths and development opportunities. At first, she recalls it was uncomfortable for both her and the employee. However, it has become part of the culture, with employees appreciating the on-going transparent feedback.

Developing Your Leadership Style and Credibility

A recent study conducted by Oracle and Future Workplace titled *AI at Work,* more than 8,300 employees worldwide were surveyed regarding their attitudes toward artificial intelligence (AI) and their managers. A whopping 64% of those surveyed indicated they trust AI more than their manager! Also concerning was that 82% believed robots could do a better job than their managers (www.prnewswire.com). This indicates a huge shift in the relationships between employees and their managers and can create real challenges for new leaders whose judgement and decisions may be questioned. When asked what a manager could do better than a robot, three areas were identified:

- Understanding feelings.
- Coaching.
- Creating or promoting a work culture.

Michael Schneider, in his article posted on Inc.com, stated as the use of AI continues to grow, managers may find their roles changing, with less focus on numbers and technical expertise and a stronger emphasis on the "soft" skills of coaching, mentoring, and engaging their employees. As a new leader, how do you develop your credibility and style in order to enhance your ability to both develop your employees and focus on the culture of the department? This section will focus specifically on building your credibility, developing an individual style, and adopting the mind-shifts needed to succeed as a new leader.

In her book, *The Credibility Code*, Cara Hale Alter shares that credibility is made up of two basic factors: competency and warmth. As a new leader, your employees will be looking for these factors as they assess you during your first few months. Just as you are assessing them, they are assessing you.

Alex and Stephanie both entered their new leader roles with what some believed to be a very visible handicap. Both had youthful looks, were younger than some of the people they managed, and had little to no leadership experience. Recognizing this challenge, Alex focused on building trust. Based on her previous experience with the company, she entered the role with some technical knowledge of the department. In her one-on-one meetings with team members, she learned about their responsibilities, what they enjoyed about their job, and what they identified as challenges. Then, she shared her expectations and working style, which included taking a supportive leadership approach. She trusted them to be the experts. She was clear that she was available if they needed assistance. Although Alex had not officially served in the role of "manager" with responsibility for direct reports, she had experience as a project manager, which required getting results by working with other people; therefore, she was able to apply many of the skills she had learned in her previous role.

Stephanie, having trained as a social worker, brought her ability to build relationships with others to her leadership role and used that skill to help build her competency. She spent time developing relationships and listening to the team. In staff huddles, she asked questions and listened to the team's feedback. The following simple questions helped her gain a better perspective of the team:

- What were they working on?
- What were the expected outcomes?
- Were there any challenges?
- What else should they be doing to add value to the organization?

Although she previously worked as a member of an experienced team, where team huddles were the norm and there was little need for one-on-one interaction with the manager, Stephanie now more fully understands every team is different. In hindsight, she wishes she had taken the time initially to have more personal contact with each team member. For Stephanie, as a team member, the personal interaction with her manager was not as important. She knew the manager was available as needed, and the team huddles provided enough information for her to do her job. In her new environment with a new and growing team, her staff members experienced new sets of challenges, with multiple areas of focus, making the need for one-on-one interactions with the leader even more essential.

A real challenge for Stephanie was determining just how many details she needed to know to do her job effectively as a director and how much she needed to know about each individual job so the team would have confidence that she understood their role and challenges. She recognized, in the end, that since she was ultimately responsible for the overall team results, it was necessary for her to find balance the between her own technical competence and the necessary confidence in the team's ability to excel.

One method new leaders use to demonstrate warmth and competence is stepping in when an employee appears to either be in need or is not producing the expected results. However, it is important to be careful to use this gift of supervisory goodwill strategically. It is important to first identify, as much as possible, the root cause for the need.

If someone is not doing their job due to performance issues, it may not be the time to step in and do the job but rather to analyze why a performance issue exists. There may be other options, such as additional training. However, if circumstances outside of the employee's control has impacted his ability to complete a project or task, it is likely the right time to step in and help.

You may have heard or even stated, "I want a manager who will work alongside me." That statement sounds good, but as a manager, you now have a different role, and focusing on producing the frontline deliverables may detract from your overall leadership responsibilities. You may be able to serve the team more effectively by building organizational relationships that create better working conditions or by securing added resources.

Both Alex and Ilona were familiar with the tasks of the department and could step in as needed, but they did so only when it became absolutely necessary. Although the team may appreciate your willingness to step in and work with them, it may also send the message that you are available to do their work whenever needed, or you lack the confidence in their ability. The "as needed" means different things to different people; therefore, staff accountability, which will be discussed later in this chapter, is important.

Developing a leadership style requires you to think critically about yourself, your individual team members, the department needs, and the culture of the organization. Every team member will approach challenges differently, have different comfort levels with the work pace, communicate differently, and have different motivations. Understanding how you, as well as your team members, prefer to operate will help you flex your leadership style as appropriate.

When beginning her management role, Alex knew that her style would have to be flexible. However, she was surprised at how much, and how often, she had to flex. For instance, she realized that demonstrating empathy was crucial. Since it was not instinctive for Alex, she had to learn about each person's style and motivation, and in some cases, even personal situations that might impact their job. She learned she had to change the tone of her voice when speaking with some of the team members. For some members of the team, being firm and straight-forward was totally expected and appropriate; for others, she had to tailor the message to be less blunt and more understanding. A management tool, such as a DISC survey, can help you learn more about yourself and your management style, as well as how others tend to address challenges, people, pace of work, and processes.

Initially, Ilona measured her employees' performance based on her personal work style and would become frustrated when others appeared to be on their phone unnecessarily, or if they appeared to not be as focused as she preferred. Recognizing that people work differently, she changed her perspective and focused on outcomes as opposed to processes. She allowed employees to approach tasks using the method that worked best for them, while she focused on outcomes. She stated, "I don't care how they get there. I don't tell them what to do, how to do it, just get there. If they need help, ask me. If they have questions, ask me. If they want me to map out the path, I'll be happy to do that, but I wasn't imposing my own path." The big challenge was giving up the ownership (but not responsibility) of how they accomplished the task and allowing others to address the assigned projects in a way that worked for them.

As part of developing a leadership style, leaders need to think and act more strategically. For some, the shift may require letting go of some of their previous tasks and even their "pet projects," which can be a struggle. In an effort not to be perceived as "dumping" tasks, new leaders may be hesitant to delegate. However, when done correctly, delegation can allow employees the opportunity to develop new skills, build trust, and improve efficiency, while allowing the leader more time to focus on the overall tasks that must be accomplished.

Accountability

In a leadership role, accountability looks different. Previously, you were measured by your contribution to the team and personal goal attainment. Now, as a leader, you are responsible for your personal goals and accomplishing team goals through others. In addition to the team goals, leaders have to consider turnover, employee engagement, and performance issues.

Ilona immediately felt the need to change her accountability perspective. She felt more was expected of her and that she needed to contribute in a new way. Part of her team worked in Asia, requiring her to gain a greater understanding of the Asian culture. Ilona, originally from Eastern Europe, was accustomed to adapting to new cultures and found many of the team members were very conscientious, understood their responsibilities, and accepted the accountability measures.

The bigger challenge was turnover. She realized some of her team members were in roles with little variation in their daily tasks. Although they were good at their job, some became bored, resulting in dissatisfaction with their role. Ultimately, some chose to pursue roles outside of the organization that provided them with better development opportunities. To encourage the employees to be more engaged, she began delegating tasks that provided variety and development opportunities for her team, which subsequently increased their satisfaction and reduced department turnover.

One leadership expectation in the hospital setting with accountability measures in place was creating a culture of safety. Each year, the organization surveyed team members regarding a culture of safety, including aspects that relate directly to the leader role. In addition, an employee engagement survey was completed annually. Based on the results, the leader is expected to build an action plan to improve that culture. Stephanie, as a leader in the hospital setting, was intentional about creating a safe environment and culture. Her steps included asking for increased input, listening to her team's ideas, and then not micromanaging her team. She saw the culture survey as not only an accountability tool for her as a manager, but a way for her to improve herself personally.

When we think accountability, often people management comes to mind; in addition, managers need to learn other accountability measures, such as budget and expense goals. They differ for each department and for each industry. Therefore, as a new leader, you need to ask about the accountability measures in your department to ensure you understand your process for success.

One area that often creates challenges for a new leader, as indicated, is the budget. If you are in a leadership role and are not familiar with the budgeting process, proactively ask questions about it, seek out managers who can help you understand its current and past status, and perhaps consider taking an online course in budgeting, accounting, or finance. In every organization, new leaders will find accountability systems in place. They should be sought out and embraced as tools for improvement, as they can be not only beneficial, but frankly, mandatory for a leader's success.

Surprise: I'm Managing During a Pandemic!

Unexpected situations as stressful as a health pandemic are tough for anyone to maneuver through, and they can add an extreme additional layer of complexity to the leadership role. Stephanie found herself in a difficult situation during the COVID-19 pandemic. Before the virus hit, her team was exceeding her expectations, meeting their performance volumes, and tracking strong with their productivity measures. A couple of months into the pandemic, and for circumstances outside of their control, some of the employees needed to be furloughed. The staff cut-back decisions were based purely on seniority, as there was no one in the department who had a performance issue.

Stephanie was not prepared to have these tough conversations with team members, especially those who were great performers. She couldn't help but ask herself, if they had stayed in another department, would they still be working? It was very tough for her to have those conversations. However, luckily, she was ultimately able to bring back all of the team, some earlier than expected. Although being a leader may sound great, recognize that you will be asked to complete some difficult tasks that may be tougher than anything you ever imagined. In these tough situations, address the tasks in a timely fashion, with authenticity, compassion, and integrity.

With the pandemic came yet another leadership surprise. The employees now had to be classified as to which were "essential," meaning they had to report to the physical location to work, and those who were "nonessential," who in many cases could work remotely from home. Alex had teams in both categories, creating fresh and unexpected challenges. For the remote teams, she had metrics to determine productivity, but she had to develop new communication methods to stay in touch. For the essential team members, her biggest challenge was to find ways to recognize their value and keep the team engaged. This situation can produce unrealistic expectations and perceptions of the workload between the essential and nonessential team members, challenging even experienced managers. Again, in these situations, be honest, understanding, and as transparent as possible.

Recommended Action Steps from Those Who Went Before You

Assess and learn before making major changes. Spend time learning about the individual team members, the overall processes of the department, and the organizational expectations of the department. Determine how to apply your skills to enhance the team and build rapport while accomplishing the team goals.

Define your relationships with your team members. When moving into a leadership role, some of your relationships may need to change; that can be done by establishing clear boundaries upfront. If you are promoted from within and have a close friend on the team, you may need to have a conversation clarifying your new role and boundaries and how it may change the relationship dynamics. Additionally, to avoid the perception of favoritism, you may also need to have the conversation at a team meeting. At times, you may receive Facebook requests from team members. When determining if you should accept the request, it is best to consider the team structure, organization, and implications or information that may be learned through Facebook posts and then weigh the costs.

Create your performance management plan. Consider how you will set expectations and how often you will meet with your staff individually or as a team. What is your staff communication plan? If you have a staff issue, what resources are available to you? Identify someone in human resources who can help you navigate the new personnel responsibilities.

Get a mentor. There will be many new skills needed for success, and a valuable way of gaining the expertise you need is through a mentor. Identify the areas where you want to improve and seek out others who are masters of that skill and ask for their advice. Learn not only the things they do well, but also from any past mistakes and lessons they will share. Write out what you want to learn (be specific), identify who has the skill and may be willing to mentor you and then send a request with your specific need and ask for help! You may be surprised at how willing people are to help when you are clear in your request.

Develop a relationship with a peer. Find a trusted peer who can support you in your new role, someone who will listen to your ideas and provide honest feedback, as well as help you navigate the organizational processes and culture. It is often valuable to have a "venting" partner who can encourage you on the tough days and help readjust your mindset when needed. Choose your "venting" partner carefully! And remember, as with any relationship, when someone has invested their time in you, be ready to reciprocate.

Flex your leadership style. Each team has unique dynamics and requires a leader who understands how to leverage their strengths. Begin by assessing the team and then think critically about yourself, your individual team members, department needs, and culture of the organization. Understand that every team member will approach challenges differently, have different comfort levels with the work pace, communicate differently, and have different motivations. Understanding how you, as well as your team members, prefer to operate will help you to flex your leadership style as appropriate.

Be humble and apologize. When you think you have made a mistake, be humble and apologize. Be open and honest about the situation, ask for understanding, learn from it, and get back to work. A sign of a great leader, as well as top employees, is how they handle mistakes. Own it, learn from it, then get back in the saddle.

Don't abuse power. Although you may have authority that comes with the title, in the long run, it is more effective to build relationships and use informal power and collaboration to get things done. Respect that everyone brings talents to the table and has expertise that can be valuable and encourage them to share their opinions. Identify someone who has been silent or hesitant to share ideas and ask for their input or perspective.

Give credit to others. Treat people with respect and give them the recognition they deserve. Recognize people individually and whenever presenting their ideas to others. The leader should share praise with the team for their contributions at the team level, as well as at the organizational level. Who do you need to recognize today?

Get comfortable with accountability. Leaders move from personal accountability to being responsible for the results of the team. When we think accountability, people management comes to mind; however, as a leader, you will also have additional accountability measures, such as budget and expense goals. Identify how you and your team will be measured and create a plan to ensure you have a method of tracking progress towards goals.

Surprise: I'm managing during a pandemic! Be prepared to address new challenges and changing situations as they arise. It's OK to ask questions and seek advice from others. In these tough situations, address the tasks in a timely fashion, with authenticity, compassion, and integrity.

Be kind to yourself. Alex Crocker stated early in her leadership role that she would beat herself up over something she said or a situation that she felt she could have handled more effectively. As a new leader, you are faced with situations that perhaps you had never discussed in class or through your actual work experiences. See it as a learning experience and provide yourself with personal forgiveness. Ilona Curry encourages new leaders to remember that no one is perfect, not even the boss! Everyday write down something that went right or something you did to make your team or organization better and celebrate!

Learn more about your leadership style by taking a quick survey at www.workplaceadvancement.com/bookclub, password nicetoknow.

Chapter 4
CHANGING BUSINESS SECTORS

Your organization is in control of your job.
You are in charge of your career.

Dr. Julie Olsen

According to the Bureau of Labor Statistics, the average person has approximately 12.3 jobs in their lifespan. Many of these job moves are in different industries and in some cases, in fields that are not the least bit similar to previous roles. The size of the organization, the profit model, and even the industry can complicate a transition, making it more difficult for someone to succeed.

People who have successfully transitioned to new industries, and, in some cases, reinvented themselves completely, followed strategies to help them succeed in new or dramatically different work environments. A focus on building trust and credibility, while being curious and learning the business as thoroughly as possible in the early weeks and months on the job, can help establish your willingness to support the team and the organization complete their objectives and ultimately contribute to your success.

This Is an Entirely New World—
Is Anything the Same?

Moving into a new industry can be quite overwhelming. Initially, it is important to assess the new environment and determine what might be similar to your previous experiences, and then, of course, what is different. That was an interesting question when talking with Stratton Leopold, who works in two different industries. What could possibly be similar between an ice cream shop and producing blockbuster movies?

Stratton grew up in the family business, Leopold's Ice Cream in Savannah, Georgia, but he was fascinated early on by the movie industry. After his dad passed away and when Stratton finished college, he returned to help with the family business. He worked with his uncle to help ensure the business continued; however, his sights were always set on moving to New York City. The ice cream business was doing well under his uncle's management, so Stratton decided it was time to make that change.

He drove to New York with no plans for what to do when he arrived. Once there, he secured a job, met an actress, found himself going to classes and auditions with her, and personally secured several roles behind the camera. As he learned more about the industry, he got the idea that he didn't want to act in movies, he wanted to produce them! But there was one huge barrier. He didn't know anything about the industry.

At that point, he made a five-year plan, realizing he had to learn everything about the business from the ground up. Although that plan had to be revised multiple times, and he did not meet most of the five-year goals in his projected timeframe, his persistence paid off. Due to his hard work and willingness to do whatever was necessary to succeed, Stratton went on to become successful in the film industry. To date, Stratton has more than 60 film and television credits to his name, including well-known movies, such as "Mission Impossible III" and "The General's Daughter." He even became the executive vice president of physical production at Paramount Pictures, which was a highly coveted position.

When Stratton was asked about the similarities in the two industries, he remarked, "They both deal with people." At the ice cream shop, he stated, "You have to enjoy meeting people and enjoy speaking with strangers. It's a family business, you're dealing with your team, and it's a happy business." However, in the film industry, "You have a team around you for a relatively short time. On large movies it may be a year, and then they are gone." He said you have to be persistent with actors and crew at times. "Developing relationships in each of these situations is different. In films, it must happen very quickly, but it is not necessarily a long-term relationship. At the ice cream shop, the relationships are deeper and last for a longer period of time. Although the nature of the relationships may differ, it's important to build them in both industries."

Growing up on a dairy farm in Pennsylvania, Karl Diffenderfer's dad taught him the value of hard work. That virtue served him well as he experimented with multiple career options that were quite diverse. While working on the farm, Karl also helped his dad run an auction house on the weekends. At age 18, he decided he did not want to go to college, and instead, he started working for a local mechanic shop. Then, about six months later, he decided to try his hand at construction. After two years in construction, his love for music led him to a position as a part-time worship leader at a small church, while he was also managing a horse farm. In the meantime, he got married and at the age of 22, his wife became pregnant, which was a major wake-up call for Karl!

He knew he finally had to get serious about his career in order to support his now-growing family. He went to a local college, obtained a graphic arts degree, and was able to combine his desire to serve the Lord with his new graphic arts education. As a new college graduate, Karl accepted a position as a graphic arts designer and youth worship minister at a large church in Pennsylvania. While in that role, he began doing freelance graphic art design work on the side, which ultimately led to a position at a large corporation. However, as time went on, he realized that what he really wanted to do was open his own business.

When the time seemed right, he stepped out on his own and opened an internet marketing agency, serving a diverse clientele that went global. In 2012, he had the opportunity to sell his business. At first, he was reluctant. However, upon considerable thought, he made the difficult decision to sell. He started "Higher IMPACT," a business and life coaching firm that works with organizations of all sizes, markets, and locations. Looking back, he learned that although each of those roles appeared different, similarities existed. Each required hard work, a commitment to do whatever was needed to complete tasks, and the ability to work with unique individuals. Today, as he consults with businesses throughout the globe, he realizes the value of each of those roles and how the lessons learned are incorporated in his current coaching practice.

Brendan Ferrara was enjoying his career in higher education. He was teaching marketing and leadership courses and ultimately rose to the level of academic dean of the Business and Professional Services Division at Savannah Technical College. After 20 successful years in higher education, Brendan was offered an opportunity to work at Savannah's "EmployAbility," a nonprofit organization that prepares adults with developmental or intellectual disabilities to gain the necessary skills to become employed in the community. With his years of teaching business skills, and his connections in the community, it seemed like the perfect fit for Brendan's next move, and he jumped at the opportunity.

Assessing the similarities and differences, he learned that moving from higher education to a nonprofit organization was not as different as he had anticipated. To his surprise, the nonprofit had many of the same constraints as government entities, and in some cases, even more, especially when it came to funding. As expected, his experience and the skills he learned in higher education had transferability to his new role and helped him to more smoothly transition into leading the in-house training enterprises at EmployAbility, such as hospitality, parts assembly, printing, graphic design, and logistics. His business knowledge also helped as he became responsible to community partners for profit and losses of those in-house business efforts, and of course, ultimately with his role as CEO.

After 30 years with a large print media organization, Stacy Jennings decided it was time for a change, and she accepted a position with a much smaller, local, family-owned, for-profit cookie company. As she looked for similarities, they were difficult to find. She immediately realized during her orientation period that the resources available in the larger organization were no longer available. In fact, very few standardized processes and limited training for new employees existed. And due to the small size of the organization, most employees had several roles.

After a short time there, Stacy decided she could better utilize her talent for marketing by opening her own consulting business. As her business grew, thanks to her superb reputation, she was asked to join the Georgia Associated Press. After multiple conversations, she agreed. Then, a position as the director of communications for the Savannah-Chatham County Public School System became available. With public education being one of Stacy's passions, she jumped at this opportunity to serve. As Stacy expressed it, "Public education is the cornerstone of our democracy." She believes education is a right for all Americans and is happy to serve the public in this role. It provides her with a sense of pride while allowing her to use the skills she learned from her many previous roles. She stated, "There's nothing more important than educating our children who are going to lead us in the future"

As you can see by these different experiences, identifying the skills you have already developed, and how those skills might be adapted and quickly transferred to your new role, will help you make a smoother transition. It will also help you contribute to your organization more rapidly and more effectively.

Shifts In the First Few Months, Or In Some Cases, Years, In Your New Role

From the farm, Karl learned that at times, you need to humble yourself and just do what needs to be done, right from the start, even if it's the dirty work. As he moved into new roles, Karl realized that although he was bright and had good ideas, he needed to take the time to learn the new organization, which meant he had to "eat humble pie" and do the "small" jobs that weren't considered glamourous. In so doing, he built relationships and began to gain the respect of those with whom he worked. He stated, "I've always been a hard worker. And I didn't realize it then, but that was giving me respect now." He feels it is vitally important that people understand this fact: "How you act right now will affect what you are later in life. And it is not what is going on outside of you. You always have a choice as to how to act, or react, in any situation." Those choices, and your willingness to work hard, especially in the first few months on the job, build your reputation and help you gain respect.

Driven to produce movies, Stratton knew expectations would be different and made intentional choices based on his goals, and those choices led to definite sacrifices. To get started in the film industry, he had to leave New York and move to Atlanta, where the film business was new and growing, providing a better chance of breaking into the industry and learning it from the ground up. While he was trying to get started, he refereed college football games so he could afford his basement apartment that leaked (more like flooded) every time it rained.

Like Karl, he knew the value of being humble and the importance of being willing to do whatever it took, even accepting entry-level jobs. And he did just that by starting at the bottom and earning almost nothing in the beginning. He took jobs behind the camera and in front of the camera and did anything that needed to be done, just to learn. He knew he needed as much knowledge as he could get about how everything worked.

He also was proactive in building his network. The president of

Universal Studios was visiting Atlanta. Before his visit, Stratton researched information about him and learned a few personal facts. He knew "Tom" was from North Carolina, so when he saw him, Stratton commented, "Tom, you're a Tar Heel," which opened a conversation and made a lasting impression on the president of Universal Studios. He followed up with, "I'm going to call you when I get to LA," which became an ongoing ritual every time he met someone in the industry. When the LA market started to open up, he made those promised calls, and after serving his "dues" in Atlanta, he was able to secure a position in LA.

Stacy learned quickly, after the first few months on her new job, that the respect she garnered over 30 years with her previous employer did not follow her to her new position. She cautions people moving into new roles to rely not on the reputation and the respect they gained from previous employers, but to focus instead on building their credibility in their new role. If the new role is in a new industry dramatically different from your previous role, that transition can be even more difficult. She stated, "You have to re-earn that respect. You've got to earn the respect while doing the things that you may not have done before." To earn the respect of her new team, Stacy focused on doing the things she does best. She would ask for help when needed, relying on the team to help her navigate her new position and the new organization. During that transition, she could see the need to let go of her control on some tasks and then allow others who were better at them complete the assignments in their own way.

Building credibility and trust were Brendan's top priorities when starting his new role at EmployAbility. Stepping into an organization that was already experiencing changes in expectations from external forces made Brendan's first few months challenging. Also, due to a family emergency, his boss had to take an extended leave for two weeks, which happened on Brendan's second day on the job.

With no clear orientation plan, Brendan simply began walking around, talking with people, and asking what they liked and didn't like about the organization. The key was just listening to them. He understood that to be successful he first needed to gain their trust. And by listening and showing a definite interest in them, he could learn more about his team and the organization. He believes, "People aren't interested in you because they think you're interesting. They're interested in you because they think you are interested in them!" He cautions that it has to be an authentic interest. Spending time getting to really know his team and the organization, and sincerely listening to their thoughts and concerns, built trust that ultimately paid off for him when difficult staffing decisions had to be made due to the COVID-19 pandemic, but more about that later.

Time to Transfer Your Skills and Learn New Ones

Stratton learned that in both the ice cream and film industries, an important skill was to work collaboratively and listen to others on the team. He recalled working on a film that already had the script and overall concept approved from a well-known major film company. As they began filming, the assistant art director had a different idea for the ending of the movie and shared it with Stratton. He took the new idea to the director, and they agreed to shoot both scripts, and, ultimately, the assistant art director's idea was used for the end of the movie.

Similarly, at Leopold's Ice Cream Shop, he listens to this team and encourages their participation in most operational decisions. His team provides input into new ice cream flavors, and Stratton accepts input from other key community and even statewide players. One of the store's new flavor, Georgia Pecan Blues, was a collaboration with his team and several agricultural and business entities throughout the state. By its name, it highlights key crops grown in Georgia. It made its debut as a fundraiser for the area United Way.

During the COVID-19 pandemic, he also looked to his team to

determine new protocols. Although the point-of-sale process in the store was redesigned and appeared to provide a safe method for customers to obtain a great scoop of ice cream, the staff recognized that a new problem had been created. The new spacing requirements for safely purchasing the ice cream took up all of the inside seating areas, leaving no place for the patrons to sit and enjoy their ice cream. Even with the store's limited outdoor space, the staff did find a way to add outdoor sidewalk seating.

According to Karl, you can learn from any job, even the bad ones, and then use those skills to be successful in new roles. Growing up on a dairy farm taught Karl the value of hard work. Working in the maintenance shop and construction taught him how to fix equipment and build structures. Helping his dad with his auctions on the weekends taught him business skills. Working at the church utilized his talent and reinforced the value of committing to something greater than yourself, which for Karl, meant his service to, and reliance on, God. The internet marketing agency required that he learn the business models of multiple organizations within diverse and often global industries, which contributed to his current success as a business and personal coach. When asked what his greatest motivator had been, he quickly stated, "The fear of not being able to provide for my family." Additionally, he had developed a strong desire to have a positive impact on the world around him. That drive created a relentless pursuit of knowledge, new skills, service, and reliance on God, as well as using those skills gained from previous jobs in new ways so that he could reach his primary goal of providing for his family.

A surprise for Karl in his early years was the realization that not everyone liked him. Growing up, he was always liked by people, and he never met anybody that he felt didn't like him. However, on the construction site, Karl recalls a big and rather rough-looking guy who clearly did not like him and seemed to do things just to make him mad. Unfortunately, it worked.

Being new to the construction world, he responded respectfully, but he was confused as to why someone would act that way. Karl finally came to grips with the fact that not everyone would like him and if that was the case, it would just have to be OK. However, it was his responsibility to learn how to work with him and if he responded negatively, it would harm his reputation and equally important, it was not in alignment with his values. He learned from the situation and chose to accept that he had to work productively with all types of people, even the difficult ones. Ultimately, Karl learned different approaches to working with diverse people, which contributed to his success.

Stacy also believes it is important to recognize the need to use your skills in a new way when you shift businesses. In particular, when she started her work with the public school system, she remembered, "I'm a marketing and branding expert, but I don't know anything about education." She took the initiative to quickly learn the new organization, reading and talking to experts in the field and asking for help when needed. However, identifying new and effective ways to apply her marketing skills learned from her previous jobs ultimately contributed to her success and made the transition much smoother.

In all likelihood, you will not know all you need to know when entering a new job or industry. "When in doubt, figure it out" was Karl's motto. As he was starting his internet marketing agency, he would be asked by clients, "Can you do this?" And he would respond with confidence, "Yes." Then, he would begin a Google search to try to figure out what he had agreed to provide. And as he did, he learned new skills along the way. If he couldn't figure it out, or if he wasn't satisfied with his solution, he would search out people who did the particular task well and ask for their help. He suggests, "Surround yourself with others that have different skills that can help you learn what you need to know, or who can assist with identifying others who can help you figure it out."

Moving into Leadership in a New Business Sector

Moving into a manager role in a new industry was a great opportunity for Brendan. Early on, he knew the CEO would be retiring in a few years, and if he learned the new industry and performed well, he would be a great candidate to become the next CEO. The retirement came much sooner than expected, and Brendan was promoted to the top position with less than two years with the new organization.

As the previous CEO's car left the parking lot on his final day on the job, Brendan felt an overwhelming weight and recalls thinking, "Now I understand the phrase, it truly is a heavy head that wears the crown." He thought to himself, "I can't do this. I'm not ready." In his previous roles, although he was the leader, he wasn't making sweeping decisions, and he had a safety net, someone else to help shoulder the responsibility. Now, people were looking to him for answers, and although he had an excellent and supportive board of directors, he was suddenly 100% responsible for the day-to-day decisions. He quickly realized, having been promoted from within, that his relationships with staff members would have to change and he had even more to learn.

As with any new role, more surprises surfaced. He learned that in the midst of all of the changes, some of the institutional knowledge had not been captured. People knew their jobs and performed them well; however, he decided it was time to record the "what's" and the "why's" of how to do each job.

To complicate the situation even more, Brendan had become the CEO just a month before the COVID-19 pandemic hit. Once the COVID-19 threat was recognized and became widespread, he had to temporarily shut down the operation. Then, he had to quickly learn how to manage the human resource implications, change processes, and redesign their entire organization, in a relatively new industry for him. Although they were already planning to make changes in their services, the pandemic accelerated the timeframe and forced his team to become quite innovative. Redesigning the entire service delivery process, including the internal training and external services, required Brendan and his team to extensively research government regulations, possible constraints, and all elements of the business before making any changes. Coming from a different sector provided him the opportunity to look at this new situation with fresh eyes. More than ever, Brendan realized the goodwill and trust that he had built in his early days on the job proved essential for the organization to reinvent itself and was critical to its survival!

Lessons Learned

Beware of mental games and be kind to yourself. Often when entering a new opportunity, you may wonder if you made the right decision. Stacy cautions people not to second guess themselves. She stated, "You can't ask yourself, what if I had done this? What if I had done that instead?" You need to commit to your new path and keep moving. When it gets tough, and it will, she says, "Put one foot in front of the other and keep going and keep things in perspective."

Learn to understand the culture, behaviors, and expectations, not only in your organization, but in the city, state, and region of the country in which you live. When Stratton moved from New York to Atlanta, he realized he had to become less aggressive. He laughs now when he shares a story of returning an item to a department store. He bought a sport coat in Atlanta, but when he got home, he realized that he didn't like it. He went back to the store to return it, with the bill of sale in hand, and he was ready for a fight. He put his receipt on the counter and stated, "I am going to return this". The clerk responded, "Yes." Stratton then replied in a firm voice, "Here's the bill of sale." The clerk responded, "Yes, it's ok." Stratton then stated, "You didn't hear me. I'm returning this. Here's my bill of sale" and continued digging further and going for the throat. Then, he realized, she was ready to refund his purchase. It wasn't a problem at all, which was not what he expected from his New York experiences! Since then, he has learned to adapt his style to the situation and culture. He uses his innate southern charm with his ice cream shop's employees but is still much more direct with one of his staff members from New York. Learning the employees, the culture, and the preferred communication style has helped Stratton be more effective as he works with his ice cream team, as well as with actors from around the globe.

Strange things happen in every organization. Brendan grew up in a police family and heard many unique situations or "strange things" that his father would experience on the job and then later share with the family. He knows people in accounting, marketing, and healthcare, all of whom can share interesting and unexpected stories. Any business dealing with the public is going to have unusual situations arise. He recommends asking veteran employees to describe their strangest encounters as a good way to anticipate what could happen and to know them when they occur.

Training opportunities are everywhere, and as you change industries, it is important to take advantage of them. Stacy shared that she "learned to learn" and spent a lot of her time brushing up on her skills and building her knowledge in every new environment. She took advantage of courses on LinkedIn that were offered by her employer. Also, Stacy made it a point to seek out resources for her development by speaking with industry experts and researching industry trends and updates. She also regularly networks with peers in the field.

Once you shift to a new organization or industry, it may not appear to be a good fit. If you are unhappy, be careful not to change positions again too quickly. Take the time to determine what is making you unhappy. The following questions might help:

- Is it the job responsibilities?
- Is it the tasks that are expected?
- Is it the manager?
- Is it the business sector itself?

Understanding the true and specific source of your frustration will help you determine if a change is really needed and then find the correct path forward. Once you have identified what bothers you the most, consider possible solutions.

- Are the things that make you unhappy within your realm of control?
- Can the issues be overcome?
- Are you receptive to looking for solutions that will make you happier in your current role?

Then, talk with your manager. Tactfully share your perspective and ask for help resolving the issues. Your manager may be able to provide additional training or possibly look at ways to redesign your role. If the issues are team-related, the manager may be able to address those personnel specific concerns.

Overall, most managers want to retain their best employees. Speaking with your manager before deciding to leave might lead to a win/win situation. If you don't discover the source of your frustration and simply move on, the same situation may well arise in your next role. Consider leaving the organization only after you have attempted to address concerns with your current manager and no real solutions have been identified.

Recommended Action Steps from Those Who Went Before You

Determine the similarities and differences. Before you decide to make a change, take the time to talk with as many people as possible. Ask about their experiences and seek their advice. Ask them what they wish someone had told them before starting. What drives the industry? What business models work best? What is the culture? Is the sector highly competitive? Is it heavily regulated? Does it serve a broad or a niche market? How many competitors are in that market? From these conversations, determine what is most likely to impact the expectations your superiors will have of you. How is the new market different from your previous experience and what might need to change?

Shifts require a passion to learn. Karl believes it was his passion, and especially his curiosity to learn, that contributed to his success as he moved through various business opportunities during his career. Be curious and actively seek to learn new information and new skills.

Know yourself. Know what is important to you. Ask if the industry you are considering matches the elements that are important to you in a job. Identify your strengths and the areas that might be a challenge for you. Take assessments and surveys and ask others for insights into how your strengths may best be used in your new setting. Know before you make a move what you like, and what you don't like in the work environment. Do you prefer to work with a team, or do you prefer to work independently? Determine what you might need to modify among your skills and preferences to be successful in a new environment. Karl discovered from his work experiences that it was, "easier for me to modify my approach than to expect other people to modify theirs." Be willing to adapt and be intentional with your career moves, ensuring that they will align well with your ultimate career goals.

Know what you are willing to sacrifice. It is important to know what you really want and expect and to be clear about it. Regardless of your employment choice, genuine success will require a laser focus. Stratton recommends knowing what you are willing to sacrifice in advance. How far do you want to go in the industry? What will be the trade-offs? Will you have to start at the bottom? What is the impact on your personal life? How might it impact your family? His passion early on was producing movies, and that required him to start at the bottom, make definite lifestyle changes, and delay family commitments.

It takes time. Look, listen, and observe. Spend time, especially in the first few weeks on the job, looking comprehensively at all that is going on in the organization. Listen to the advice from the team, and of course, the instructions from your manager. Be approachable and teachable. Focus on winning the trust of those with whom you will work. Determine how you can apply your skills to the new environment.

You must build trust. Building goodwill and trust in the very beginning as a leader will lay a foundation of collaboration which will be extremely beneficial when the inevitable "surprises" surface. What is your strategy to build trust with your new team?

There is much to learn so ask for help. As with any new role, it is important to seek the help you need. Even if you come with extensive experience, it is tempting to move forward as if the things that made you successful elsewhere will work in your new role. However, that might not be the case. Although it may be true in some situations, you may need to gain new skills and adapt others. Take the time to observe the organization, learn the culture, and ask a lot of questions. If you are unsure, it is far better to ask for the help you need, demonstrating a willingness to learn. By so doing, you will build relationships and trust with the team.

To enhance your leadership in a new setting, download the *10 Important Qualities for Effective Leadership at Work Action Guide* at www.workplaceadvancement.com/bookclub, password nicetoknow.

Chapter 5
BUSINESS IS BUSINESS RIGHT?

"Change begins at the end of your comfort zone."

Roy T. Bennett

As people begin their career, often they will start with a revenue model, whether it be nonprofit, for-profit, or government services, and they stay with that model throughout their career. However, sometimes people switch from nonprofit to for-profit models or the reverse. Although there are similarities, "sector bending" has gained in popularity (referring to the blurring of lines between models), with differences between the models remaining and impacting the work experience. People who switch profit models learn quickly that what made them successful in the previous model may not lead to success in the new environment, and once again, adaptation is key. Quickly learning the differences posed by the new business model will help you avoid some of the land mines that could sabotage your success and help you become both productive and valued much faster.

Lisa Shumate experienced many transitions throughout her career in the media. She began as a reporter, served as an anchor for a local television news station, and then worked on the business side in marketing and programming. As an accomplished media executive with more than 20 years of experience in the for-profit media sector, Lisa had the opportunity to become the associate vice president and general manager of Houston Public Media, the local public broadcasting station.

After working in the for-profit world for her entire career, Lisa found new skills she needed to learn on the nonprofit side. One of the biggest changes she experienced was understanding the different business model. She went from an advertising sales-based revenue model to an education television model, one that was supported not through the sale of commercials, but through grants and donations. Her organization also received support through government services (e.g., infrastructure and human resources from the associated public university). Her biggest learning curve was figuring out how to successfully navigate the complexities of working in an institutional environment that had a separate 501 (c)(3) board of directors. In her words, "There's a lot of people to please, a lot of people to check with to be sure you are not inadvertently going off a policy that is there for a reason." At first, she perceived many of the practices as somewhat bureaucratic but later realized that the processes were necessary and provided organizational stability.

Starting her career in banking, Kim Barnhill knew she wanted to help people and for her, that came in the way of assisting them with their personal finances. She helped with everything from starting a banking account to financing a home to investment planning. In addition to her banking role, she served on the board of directors for the local food bank. Kim was impressed with the leadership and the business model, so when she was asked to consider the position of development director, she agreed.

Once she made the transition, she recalls thinking, "No one could prepare me for what I walked into, which was COVID! As the Chief Development Officer, I was hired to develop awareness through marketing and fund-raising initiatives, but then the world changed and along with it, my scope of work. My focus shifted to manpower and getting food to people in need. It was overwhelming and there was nothing to do, but just roll your sleeves up and jump in. Accordingly, Kim found herself working and managing a part of operations to help meet the needs of the organization. After a year in the non-profit industry, Kim was presented with a banking opportunity. Although it was an extremely tough decision, Kim decided to move back into the banking world to continue her personal development.

Throughout her career, Honor Lind worked with both nonprofit and for-profit entities. She experienced many differences in the revenue models, each with distinct cultures requiring different motivations and work styles, and she found similarities as well. Both were mission-driven, but the availability of resources impacted how each approached fulfilling the mission.

At one point, Honor moved from a small nonprofit organization to a much larger for-profit business. She recalls that both were fast paced in different ways. With her nonprofit experience, she was required to think like an entrepreneur and solve problems with limited resources and outdated technology that increased the workload (and her workday). Much of her focus was on fundraising. In her for-profit experience, technology was seen as a highly valued investment, reducing some of the administrative and tracking expectations and providing data in real-time. One of the hardest parts of moving to the for-profit sector was learning to navigate the systems and the increase in productivity expectations made possible by the new technology.

In addition to the three previous people who were interviewed, information was gathered through confidential interviews with healthcare executives in the hospital setting who had transitioned between nonprofit and for-profit healthcare organizations. Learning the culture and criteria for success was a common theme. Some of the primary similarities included, of course, a focus on patient care while operating in a highly regulated industry, with complicated payment sources, and the need to be financially stable to survive. As for differences, for-profit entities not only serve the community, but they must ensure a return to their shareholders in the form of profits. Nonprofits need to be financially stable to ensure they can fulfill their mission and report to stakeholders instead of shareholders. Their profits are required to be reinvested into services that enhance the community. These differences often result in different cultures, tracking systems, incentives, and accountability measures that need to be understood as someone transitions to an entirely new revenue model.

Be a Student of Culture

Many of us have an idea of what it might be like to work in a different revenue model. However, Honor recommends not assuming your perceptions are reality. It is important to understand the culture, language, and roles and responsibilities of your position and others in the organization. When transferring to a for-profit entity, Honor thought she would have a similar scope of responsibility as she did in her nonprofit role, just on a greater scale.

In the nonprofit world, due to limited resources and the small size of the organization, Honor was responsible for a holistic approach to her role, meaning, if something needed to be done to satisfy the client, she had the authority to do it, even if it was not in her direct line of responsibility. In the larger for-profit organization, departments and responsibilities were much more defined, as were expectations. If something fell outside of her department, other departments were available for support, and they would accept responsibility and meet the customer's need.

Kim experienced more definition in the for-profit model related to career paths and development. She recalls being oriented to the banking structure, the jobs available throughout the organization, management expectations, and career pathways in her early days with the bank. "It's clear; you know how to get from A to B to Z." In the nonprofit, when opportunities were available, there was more flexibility. The flexibility was good in one sense; however, the clarity regarding where and how to advance was not as clear. Sometimes positions were grant funded and therefore not considered permanent, making it harder to depend upon that path for career development.

Clearer lines of responsibilities and expectations were also discussed in the interviews with healthcare executives. In the for-profit hospital systems, the responsibilities and expectations were clear and standardized across the organization. One leader summed it up by stating that you know what you are expected to do and "you need to stay in your lane." Similar to Honor's nonprofit experience, in the nonprofit hospital setting, many of the leaders referenced the need to look holistically at their service and were expected to take ownership of opportunities, collaborating as necessary, even if it was not their direct responsibility.

The media industry appeared to have similar differences. With commercial media, Lisa said, "Everyone understands they're getting paid to make money for the organization, the shareholders, or the owners. It's very clear. In nonprofit organizations, people are equally focused on the mission." These different perspectives create different work experiences and a different pace for decision-making.

For healthcare administrators, the pace and rate of change were differentiators as well. With clear expectations and strong tracking systems, for-profit hospitals appeared quicker to adjust or change. One leader expressed it this way: "I don't think the for-profits pull any punches, and they make financial changes quickly, because they are for-profit, and they have stockholders. Nonprofits have the same focus, the same financial concerns. They just can't turn the ship as fast."

Leadership focus was also identified as different between the two revenue models. In the nonprofit hospitals, senior leaders were more externally focused, analyzing methods of increasing connectivity with businesses and organizations in the community. For-profit hospitals were typically larger, with decisions made at the corporate level. As such, leaders at the hospital level were more internally focused on bottom-line performance and internal operations. Decisions were based on data with less room for individual customization as might be more likely in some small nonprofit hospitals.

Applying What You Know While Learning New Knowledge

With limited resources in her nonprofit roles, Honor found the abundance of sophisticated technology in the for-profit environment to be a challenge. Luckily, she was a quick learner and took the initiative to gain the technology skills she needed. In both settings, Honor felt she could apply her passion and recognized how she could apply previous skills to a new setting. She stated, "In the nonprofit, you are trained to see opportunities, make connections, and create solutions." She was able to apply that training to her for-profit experience by quickly offering solutions and breaking down department barriers. The for-profit experience taught her cutting-edge business practices and technology that she has been able to apply and share with nonprofit entities.

Similar to Honor, Kim found that the skills she gained through her for-profit experience were valuable in her new nonprofit role. Coming from a more structured environment, Kim was able to analyze processes and introduce new concepts and procedures. Specifically, she implemented new tracking systems for the Volunteer Center, which enhanced its ability to know exactly what needed to be packed, where the shipments were going, and what foods were leaving the center at any given time. She used her networking skills to build trust with her peers and the community early on. In addition, coming from a sales culture where motivation was key, she was able to inspire the nonprofit team and help them understand the value they bring not only to the organization, but to the entire community.

Lisa found herself in a situation where she underestimated how big the job would be, which ended up providing her with multiple surprises. Her first big difficulty was due to her confidence in her skills. She believed she understood what was needed in her new role and stopped seeing the need to learn new skills. But, when she got here, she realized new challenges would require new skills. At one point she admitted, "I felt at a loss and wondered if I could succeed in the job. I probably should have asked more questions in the interview, but I can't dwell on that." She then made a conscious decision to just figure it out.

Her experiential learning included making a few bad hiring decisions before she learned to take her time and ensure she was recruiting the right person. She said, "Commitment is more important than expertise because it's the commitment that keeps you going and feeds the energy to overcome obstacles." Even though she was in her fifties, and in a top media job, she sought to expand her horizons by completing an MBA program. It had been her goal for many years, and it was the role transition that pushed her into action. It was an investment in herself that she is proud to have accomplished. She encourages everyone to continue to learn. If formal education isn't for you, there are a lot of free offerings online, and you can learn from other people. To be successful, never stop investing in yourself.

An additional area that Lisa believes is important to learn is the need to understand your funding sources. Lisa's organization already had some funding sources, but it was an entirely new revenue model for her. Her commercial experience was transactional. People would buy ads and the station would run them.

With the nonprofit, she received government funding and donations. Government grants come with a lot of reporting requirements, so you have to understand the expectations attached to a grant. With large fundraising events, you need good event management skills and must stay keenly aware of the ticket sales and event plans. Lisa stated, "You are talking about people making a gift in return for recognition." And memberships add another dimension. Lisa discovered philanthropy is complex and personal. "It's very different," she said. Early on, she made the mistake of not realizing the relationship-building necessary to maintain and grow individual giving. With more than 50,000 donors, she realized quickly that she needed to understand the donors at all levels. Some were first-time donors, and some may not have been giving a lot but had been consistent for many years and needed to be celebrated. In addition, she needed to be intentional about meeting with top-level donors and understanding their motivations. This was a whole new world!

The Leader Experience and Accountability

Although both the nonprofit and for-profit organizations have their mission as a priority, nonprofits focus on community needs to drive decisions, with corporate and local input. For-profits use a systems approach, with heavy influence on delivering profit goals, and decision making, processes, and guidance are provided by a corporate office. Processes are more standardized in for-profit hospitals with clear expectations and business operating procedures. One healthcare executive stated, "The systems make managing the people easier. The expectations are clear with transparent tracking mechanisms. Therefore, everyone knows who is producing and who is not."

According to the healthcare executives in the for-profit setting, clear expectations, coupled with more sophisticated reporting mechanisms to track goals, productivity, and outcomes, create strong accountability measures. The massive data available identifies deviations quickly and serves as the framework for accountability. Clearly expressed expectations and transparent tracking systems provide the manager with the tools needed to manage to their targets. One leader stated, "There are clear achievable goals, and they reinforce those goals daily." Another leader described it as "accountability on steroids!" The leaders that were successful in this environment felt that leaders like it because they see the accountability. They see they get rewarded and recognized.

Outside of healthcare, but still in the for-profit arena, Honor found a similar type of accountability. Productivity was tracked in real-time, expectations and goals were clear, and rewards for accomplishments were also clear. Lisa concurred. In the commercial media industry, the resources and outcomes were tracked and available in real-time. In her nonprofit experience, they were still building the data capacity to have timely reporting. For Kim, fewer systems and less structure related to accountability in the nonprofit environment provided more discretion at the leadership level for dealing with behavior.

Nonprofits in healthcare rely on tracking mechanisms; however, the sophistication varies by organizational size. The smaller they are, the less likely they are to have prescriptive processes and systems in place to track metrics as effectively and timely as for-profit hospitals. When expectations aren't met, leaders may be provided some leniency regarding how and when to get measures back on track based on local conditions that impact results.

Lisa, Kim, and Honor all agreed that the systems available to them in the nonprofit sector were not as robust as those in for-profit organizations, making real-time tracking more difficult. However, they felt a keen sense of accountability to the community, as they were spending money provided by people who were committed to the mission, as opposed to the transactional exchange in the for-profit arena, where the buyer and seller gain something tangible from the transaction.

Healthcare leaders shared that retention strategies are important for both profit models. For-profit hospitals tended to survey employees more frequently, often each quarter, and leaders were expected to respond to identified opportunities to improve their environment (and productivity). Nonprofit hospitals also surveyed employees with an expectation for improvement; however, the survey was typically completed on an annual basis.

Recognition was also important in both arenas, yet they approached it differently, with nonprofits focusing on personalized, mission-driven, and often nontangible recognition, while for-profits took a more standardized approach and focused on tangible programs based on the mission and results-driven measures. Incentives varied by profit model as well. In for-profit hospitals, leaders were incentivized through bonuses and often through competition. Goal completion and outcomes were published systemwide, so a leader could see their personal and team results in comparison to other leaders and teams in the organization. Of course, no one wanted to be at the bottom of the list!

Honor said tangible incentive programs were offered at the for-profit organizations where she worked. She recalled, "You could get another 5% commission if you exceeded a goal, and you might get a bonus as well. In addition, you might get days off, coffee, doughnuts, and all types of food." In the nonprofit, she remembered being incentivized by leaving a legacy and with other intangible rewards.

Even with the differences between sectors, today there is a move towards sector-bending. Sector-bending is when nonprofits and for-profits begin to behave in a similar manner or in the same service area. With market changes, nonprofits are forced to have more of a focus on financial performance and function much like their for-profit peers. The main difference is with the funding sources and how the profits are used.

Nonprofits reinvest their "profits" back into the organization and services for the community. For-profit organizations often return their profits to added equipment and services as well as to shareholders. Kim stated, "No matter what business you're in, if it's a good business, and it's well run, ultimately, it's all about the bottom line. In the nonprofit world, ultimately you can't help people without continuing to increase the bottom line."

Sector-bending became very real for Lisa. She was told when she was hired to bring more of a business approach to the nonprofit world. The community now expects nonprofits to demonstrate their worth and their value. Lisa faced the difficult challenge of transforming a philanthropic culture into one that also understood the business. In other words, she had to translate business needs into mission language.

Lisa's journey transforming the culture was not without its challenges, and they began early. As her boss was introducing her to the team, he mispronounced her name and totally messed it up to the point that it was not recognizable. Her new employees were googling her and began to wonder why she couldn't be found! She also recalls being viewed as an outsider. "I'm sure their feeling was they needed me to adapt. I was the new one. And I feel like I did need to learn a lot," she remembered. Her employees were going to need to change as well. She took the time to learn from the team and began taking steps to build trust. She knew without complete trust, implementing change would be far more difficult.

As with any transition, it is important to understand how your skills will transfer from one revenue model to another and how the work experience will change. Moving from the nonprofit environment to the for-profit environment will require a focus on applying the skills you have, while learning new skills, often at a faster pace, and with different expectations and strong accountability systems. Moving from the for-profit to the nonprofit environment will require a strong focus and connection to the mission and a good understanding of the organization's governance and learning a new and often quite complex funding model.

Recommended Action Steps from Those Who Went Before You

Be a student of culture. Determine the business drivers, measurements of success, and nuances that are different from your previous revenue model. In both models, be ready to learn the culture. Learn the language, communication norms, pace, expected outcomes, roles of others in the organization, and how other roles impact your responsibilities.

Reflect on the things that went well and those that could have gone better. Keep a learning log, which is simply a journal to capture your experiences and what you learned. Consider how you can continue to capitalize on those things that went well. For the things that might have gone better, identify what you could have done to improve the outcome. What would you do differently next time?

Be ready for change. When changing revenue models, there will be significant changes, not only in how you function from day to day but in the definition of success. In your first few weeks on the job, identify who is successful in their roles and what they do that contributes to their success. What are the tracking mechanisms in place and how do they relate to your role? One leader commented that you have to let go of the old and embrace the new.

Leadership expectations and the governance model will be different in different revenue models. If you are in a non-profit organization, there will be a board of directors. Learn who they are, their businesses, what is important to them, and how you can support their objectives. Perhaps there is a greater expectation of community involvement outside of your defined duties. If you move to a for-profit entity, determine where decisions are made. Is there a corporate office? Or is it a smaller, locally owned entity? Are decisions allowed to be made at the local level? Again, determine what is important to the decision makers and identify how you can support their objectives.

Determine where you fit in the organization. It is important to determine how you can best support the overall organization. Find out not only how you fit into the greater organizational matrix, but what level of decision-making you have, vital department collaborations needed, and your internal and external customers.

You will make mistakes. Learn from them! Lisa says to expect mistakes. Whether you are working in the for-profit or nonprofit model, the environment is new and you will not be perfect. Pick yourself up and keep going. Consider what happened and what you might do differently if that situation arises again. Add your observations to your learning log. In addition, if possible, find a colleague, an "encouragement partner" if you will, who can help you move on and most importantly, grow!

Download Resilience: 7 Skills You Need to Succeed During a Transition Checklist at www.workplaceadvancement.com/bookclub, password nicetoknow.

Chapter 6
INTO THE CIVILIAN WORLD

*48% of veterans indicate their transition
is more difficult than expected.*

www.military-transition.org

Approximately 200,000 service members transition from military service to the civilian world each year, according to a summary of *Transitioning Service Members Fast Facts* on the U.S. Government Accountability Office website. Of the 200,000 who transition, about 44% (or 88,000) of them leave their first job in less than a year (Pew Research). Transitioning from military life to the civilian workplace may be a shock, and it may challenge one's understanding of the corporate world. However, a focus on learning and an interest in the business can help overcome a lack of knowledge or experience in the industry. After speaking with military service members who successfully transitioned to the civilian world, several strategies emerged that led to their success.

Army Lieutenant Colonel Bill Golden, a retired U.S. Army special operations aviator, who served with task force 160, the Night Stalkers, and has a degree in finance from the University of Alabama, transitioned from battalion command of a special operations aviation battalion to banking executive in New York City. He quickly learned that he "didn't know much" about the industry and made learning a priority. As he started his new role in banking, he soon noticed a few stark differences between the military and the civilian world. One of his first observations was the difficulty of knowing who was in charge. In the military, everyone wore their rank on their uniform, making it easy to identify who was the ultimate decision-maker and leader. In the civilian world, an employee badge may provide a hint as to who is in charge; however, it is more likely that there is shared leadership and decision-making, depending on the goal.

Growing up in a small rural area in Oregon, John Wheeler readily admits that he had limited exposure to people outside of his community. While attending his brother's Navy boot camp graduation, he was amazed at the number of people at the graduation, as well as the diversity of the group. "As crazy as it may sound, I never saw anyone other than white people." John was in total awe of the different cultures and the opportunity to meet so many people.

Upon returning home, he told his dad, who was ex-Navy, that he was ready to enlist. And he did. During boot camp, they showed a movie about "the cream of the crop," the Navy Seals. John had the opportunity to take the qualification physical test, passed, and joined the ranks of the Navy Seals. He stated, "There is nothing better than working faster and being a part of that team." When he transitioned to the civilian world, he noticed two very different elements: one, the speed of accomplishing the mission was not as quick, and two, the depth of the relationships at work varied. He built good relationships as a civilian but said that none of them compared to the camaraderie on the Seal team. He grew to understand that although the relationships in the civilian world were strong, they would always be different. After the military, John spent four years in the financial industry and realized that finance was not his passion. Ultimately, he purchased Pure Water Bottling, which has grown into a successful water bottling company in California.

Lonnie Harrison, a 31-year recently retired Coast Guard captain, moved into a civilian maritime regulatory consulting position with a large regional corporation. His perception of leaders in the corporate world was more like the monopoly guy with a monocle, smoking big cigars and playing a lot of golf. He soon learned nothing could be further from the truth and that corporations run on tight margins, with money ruling the day.

Although the Coast Guard, the smallest of the armed services, had limited financial and organic resources, Harrison recalled that he could always effectively get missions accomplished by leveraging resources from federal, state, local, and private entities by citing common goals and interests. In the corporate world, as he quickly discovered, those partnerships did not exist, as other entities were competitors. With profit margin on the forefront to keep the organization viable, tough strategic operational decisions had to be made regarding what realistically could be accomplished and what had to be sacrificed due to funding restrictions.

During his 21-year career in the Air Force, Brantley Player grew his technical expertise in civil engineering. He was promoted to multiple leadership positions, with his last assignment as director (superintendent) of pavement, structural and heavy repair. Brantley's preparation for his transition to the civilian world began by learning more about business before he left the military. While serving, Brantley took advantage of the educational support offered by the military and completed his undergraduate degree, an MBA, and several well-recognized business certifications to prepare him to bridge the gap between military service and the private sector.

After leaving the military, Brantley landed a position as a project manager with a mechanical contractor. One major difference he noticed early in his new leadership role was how you deal with an underperformer was quite different. In the military, underperformers were moved typically into a lower position where they could still be useful. In a private company, the choices are different. If someone is not performing, Brantley said, "I have the authority to fire someone and they also have the ability to quit." This new environment requires different leadership.

Ken Harrison, a retired Marine Major who served on active duty and in the Reserves, was surprised by how the difference in focus between the military and the civilian environment impacted everyday operations. The Marines demonstrate an unwavering commitment to their assigned mission. According to Ken, expectations and goals were clear, understood by all, and a priority, and everyone was laser-focused and willing to sacrifice personally to achieve success. As a result, everyone would work together to get the job done, regardless of their personal feelings towards others on the team. In comparison, employees in the civilian world may have varying levels of commitment to the goal, creating an atmosphere where relationship issues can serve as a distraction to the true needs of the organization and may ultimately impact the organizational success.

Starting Over

A common theme among those interviewed was the need to consider the new civilian role as starting over in a sense. Bill Golden went from being the leader at the head of the table at a meeting, with great influence and a deep understanding of the operation, to the outer ring, where he was not even sure what the leaders were discussing at times. It was quite humbling. He knew he was hired because they believed he was a good "fit," however, he had a lot to learn about the industry.

In the beginning, he thought he would show up, be the first one there, work hard, and listen to others. Since this strategy worked for him in the past, he relied on his ability to learn quickly. In hindsight, he knows now that he should have tried to learn more about the organization and the industry before starting his new job.

John transitioned out of the military during a time when not as many opportunities existed, and he knew he had to reinvent himself. He learned the financial industry and became a financial broker only to realize that the financial industry was not his passion. While taking a few classes at the local college, he studied water bottling and discovered it was a $40 billion industry and growing.

Then, one of his financial clients discussed the possibility of selling his bottling business, which piqued John's interest. He researched the company, the competition, and the industry and created a business plan, which resulted in John buying the business. With no previous knowledge of owning a business or the water bottling industry, John found that he was much more fulfilled owning his own company, and he was very good at it. Every six months, he was doubling his business.

Lonnie also had a huge learning curve. In his final position as captain in the Coast Guard, Lonnie commanded multiple Coast Guard stations, worked with more than 100 federal agencies, and was responsible for approximately 750 people. Leaving the service, he transitioned to a small organization to lead a team of five, with each member of the team having more than 20 years of experience in their respective roles.

Moving from a large span of control, 31 years of experience, and confidence in his role to a small organization where his team had more industry knowledge and expertise than he did was mentally challenging and more than a little intimidating. It required a shift from leading and relying on others with strong expertise to becoming a subject-matter expert himself. He had to make a shift from mentor to mentee and be comfortable asking questions of his team and others. His leadership style quickly shifted from sole commander to being more inclusive. Now, everyone on the team is more aware of the other team members' priorities and everyone has a voice. With two years of experience in his new role, Lonnie admits he still has plenty to learn and is grateful for the support of his team as he continues to learn.

Brantley was responsible for teams of up to 160 people before he moved to a small team in the private sector. In the Air Force, with a defined team, when he needed more manpower, he always had the opportunity to "borrow" from others at no additional expense. He also could lend out his available manpower to other units in need. In the private sector, the manpower may be "borrowed" from another business unit; however, the associated costs are transferred to his department. This concept was new to Brantley and required him to consider projects and costs in a new manner.

Regardless of your transition, be prepared to assertively accept and confront your need for substantial learning. Although the organization may provide some training, it will be up to you to aggressively pursue the information needed for your success. Learn as much as you can about the industry, your organization, its culture, and the technical elements of the role, and don't stop when you become comfortable.

The industry and the organization are constantly changing, making it imperative that you continue to stay up to date on trends and changes. Realize that this learning curve may be reflected in your initial salary, so be realistic in your expectations and understand that your salary will most likely increase with your experience and knowledge. As you continue to grow, part of the learning will come from being open to advice from others within your organization and from contacts in the industry. You do not have to be the expert in everything on day one and, you may not ever be the expert.

In the initial days, Bill Golden realized that he had to listen to those with more experience and consider the actions they suggested he do, versus what he instinctively thought he should do. By adhering to the advice of experienced leaders in the organization and others in the industry, he was able to effectively navigate the new culture. Another method of getting up to speed quickly is to find a mentor. Some organizations will assign a mentor; however, it may be beneficial to seek out additional mentors (as discussed in Chapter 1). It is expected with any new role that there will be a learning curve; therefore, it is normal to need and seek help. Do not be shy about asking for the assistance you need. Your employer expects it.

Cultural Shifts

Even though each branch of the military has a different culture, every branch has unique qualities and some similarities with other branches. Commonalities include extensive planning, structure, accountability, and clear communication. On the civilian side, each organization also has a unique culture that may be quite different from the military, making the transition more challenging. Therefore, transitioning to the civilian world requires acknowledging and understanding the differences. The often-found differences between the military and the civilian work environment highlighted in this section include planning, structure, communication, and receptivity to change (which is no longer accomplished by "command").

Planning was an area that was quite different for Bill. As a Night Stalker, he said, "We planned incessantly down to the very finite degrees. In fact, we would plan every contingency three levels deep. We would know, if I don't have gas here, then I've got an option get it from here. And if that didn't work, I've got an option here." He was surprised planning was not as extensive in the business world, and it took him time to fully understand why. He did not gain an appreciation of the civilian planning process until he had a better understanding of the business and the culture. In a new organization, take the time to learn the planning process, as well as the rationale for the different approaches to planning.

For John, planning was also part of his Navy Seal training. He echoed Bill's experience on "what ifs." He said, "Before you go on a mission, you 'what if' everything. It doesn't matter what it is, you 'what if' it". Being true to his training, John wrote his business plan accordingly. He included everything he imagined that could go wrong and what he would do in each situation. It was fluid, which helped as he began to grow his business. He changed it several times in his first few years and now has a strong business as a result.

For Ken, the structure and formality in the Marines provided ease when it came to accountability. With similar motivation, everyone was focused on the mission, and the lines of authority and the consequences for not meeting expectations were clear. In the business arena, the methods of dealing with accountability may be unclear, with each organization creating its internal standards.

In Lonnie's situation, he was dealing with a highly educated team that was extremely competent, making accountability less of an issue and his previous military title less relevant. Bill found his military rank and experience were only valuable through his first interview process and job. He stated, "After that, you have to understand the organization and the structure and learn how to navigate the interwoven organizational complexities while delivering on your own assigned role expectations." No longer can you rely on your previous rank or authority for credibility. Your credibility will come from consistently delivering professional results.

Organizational and interpersonal communication is also different. You will have to learn new terms, acronyms, and communication styles. Again, communication in each organization will differ, although expect the style, process, and channels to be dramatically different from the accepted direct military style. After receiving feedback that his communication style came across as confrontational at times, a mentor within the organization helped Bill see how his military training was evident in his direct emails and formal meeting style. His mentor helped him consider alternative views and a less direct, yet still effective, method of communication, which resulted in greatly increasing his collaboration with others throughout the organization.

John soon realized that not only was the communication style different, but the civilian work mentality also was different, and it took him time to understand it. In the military, rank provided direction, and you didn't question it. In the civilian world, it is important to get input from your team, listen to their concerns, and gain commitment to the goals. Also, as a Navy Seal, John was accustomed to working odd hours and completing a mission, no matter the time it took. It took him time to be comfortable with the civilian lifestyle of going to work at a regular time and having coffee breaks, established lunchtimes, and a departure time dictated by a clock. It was a huge shift from his experience as a Navy Seal.

For Brantley, the perspective of determining a career path was the biggest cultural surprise and shift. Determining a career path in the military was rather clear. Early in his career, Brantley determined what he wanted to achieve and crafted his career path. Over time, through development and mentorship, he obtained his goals. In the private sector, he has had difficulty determining next steps and found that paths are not always as clear as they were in the military, and they may take many turns.

Change is expected in all organizations; however, the rate of change and rate of employee acceptance of change is dependent on the business and industry. In the Coast Guard, Lonnie experienced a culture of great resilience. Situations and conditions were constantly changing, often mid-stream, making change a common mindset. Knowing this from their past and on-going experience, the team was very adaptable and accepting. Depending on the organization, change may not be as prevalent, making even minor changes more difficult.

Coming from a military background, recognize others on the team may not have experienced the same level of urgency, stress, and change as you experienced during your military service. Therefore, focus on keeping things in perspective and helping others to do the same. Learn the reasoning behind the change and help others to then see why a particular change is necessary. Look for ways to visibly support the change and motivate others to do the same.

Adding Value

With the learning curve comes a varying degree of your ability to add value to the organization at the beginning. When you start, you typically are costing the organization money as they orient and train you for your role. Although the value you add right out of the gate may seem minimal, over time, that value will increase. In the average organization, it takes 12-18 months for someone to reach the point of fully contributing. The good news is there are ways to accelerate your contribution level. Here are a few examples.

Ken and John both said an immediate contribution you can make is to ensure you continue those same basic professional behaviors learned in the military. Do not underestimate the importance of soft skills and consistency. As before, show up to your job on time or early and wear the right "uniform," whatever that may be in your organizational culture. Be clean and sharp and pay attention to the little things. In the military, you had to get up at a certain time, be in formation at a certain time, and complete your mission at a certain time. It is the same in the business world. You are expected to be punctual, prepared to work, and deliver timely results. Set a strong example of commitment from the beginning and recognize that you are not only accomplishing the productivity expected for the organization, but also building your career reputation.

Another strategy is to become active in the organization. Get involved in employee groups, company initiatives that support the community, and appropriate after-work activities. Determine how you can use your expertise and skills to add value to initiatives that are important to your organization. Bill knew building relationships with the military and military recruitment were important to his organization. He joined their military support group and within a year, due to his leadership and strong organizational skills, he was running it. If you can't immediately contribute to your satisfaction or expectation in your hired role, find another avenue to help the organization succeed, while simultaneously building your personal and professional value to the organization.

Most people join the military with a desire to serve. For personal fulfillment after leaving the military, look for ways to serve the community. After a 20-year career of service in the Marines, Ken felt a loss of purpose and searched for ways to continue to serve his community in new ways. He joined the Legislative Advocacy Group for the Society of Human Resource Management where he could use his expertise and experience to advocate for policies that can positively impact veterans. He joined the Navy League and other community organizations where he felt he could have an impact. Seek out ways to use your talents and continue to serve and contribute to society in new ways.

Networking

What comes to mind when you hear the word networking? For many people, it has a negative connotation. However, in today's world, it is a necessity. Amanda Augustine, Career Expert at TopResume.com, defines networking as simply establishing and nurturing long-term, mutually beneficial relationships with the people you meet. According to Tiziana Casciaro, Francesca Gino, and Maryam Kouchaki in their article *Learn to Love Networking* published in the *Harvard Business Review*, professional networks can improve the quality of your work and your capacity to innovate. Networking within your company can help you gain a broader organizational perspective, learn about other departments, and identify resources that can help you be successful. Networking externally can build industry expertise and may lead to knowledge sharing and additional collaborations.

Lonnie started networking before he left the military by identifying others who were transitioning to the civilian world and staying in touch with them. He suggests that when you decide to leave military service, identify people who are leaving or have already left and stay in touch. They may become great assets or mentors as you establish and maneuver through your new career, especially if they are in the same industry that you are pursuing.

Brantley had similar advice. He used informational interviews to learn about different career possibilities. Like Lonnie, he spoke with veterans who transitioned in the last 3–5 years to seek their advice. He cautions to be careful whom you ask and recommends they have the experience that will help you with your goals. If you want to enter a completely different civilian role, find others who have successfully transitioned into something similar. If you want a civil servant role, then seek people who left the military to become a civil servant with the Department of Defense. To challenge your thinking, Brantley suggests mentoring resources that can be found on Verterati.com and follow veterans such as Michael Quinn, Matt Quick CDN-P, and Charles Wells SPHR on LinkedIn.

With your new organization, continue to network within and outside of your department. Who you associate with can open doors and multiply your effectiveness. Bill found that building his network of people and relationships throughout the organization added leverage and resulted in greater accomplishments for him and his colleagues. He maintained the mindset that these were reciprocal relationships that provided him the opportunity to meet people at all levels of the organization and understand what had to happen to move objectives forward. In return, he would find ways to help others meet their objectives.

For Ken, joining and leveraging professional associations was quite valuable. Identifying industry groups or professional organizations related to your new role and getting involved can broaden your knowledge and lead to a better understanding of how you can have an impact. Look for trade shows, luncheons, conferences, or online groups that provide an opportunity to interact with others in your industry.

Building a strong network in your organization and outside of your organization can be one of the most powerful strategies you can employ. In the *Harvard Business Review* article, *Learn to Love Networking*, four strategies are identified to ease discomfort and enhance your networking skills.

> • First, focus on learning. Consider networking as an opportunity to gain new insight or discover something new.
>
> • Second, when meeting someone new, focus on identifying goals or interests that are in alignment with yours and build authentic meaningful conversations around commonalities.
>
> • Third, reciprocate. Find ways to help others in your network and especially those who have invested in you.
>
> • Fourth, remember there is a higher purpose for networking. Think about how it will not only help you, but how it can help others on your team or in your industry. Do you have a special cause that may benefit if you have a broader network?

Finding ways for your network to be beneficial to others can help you overcome some of your hesitations, misconceptions, and barriers to networking.

Building a broad network has multiple benefits and can be a powerful tool for your personal development and career advancement. It can help you learn valuable industry trends, provide you with organizational knowledge, and identify career opportunities in your organization. Recognizing that many people tend to shift jobs over time, networking can also help you identify opportunities in your industry or in a new industry. If you are in a leadership role, networking can help build your team competencies or identify and attract good talent. Maintaining a strong network internally can provide insight into strategic organizational changes and build your ability to contribute and influence outcomes. It is well worth the investment!

Recommended Action Steps from Those Who Went Before You

Whether you completed four years of military service or retired after 20–30 years, success in the civilian world will look quite different from your military experience. Jocko Willink, in his book *The Code. the Evaluation. the Protocols: Striving to Become an Eminently Qualified Human*, shares that no matter what your new transition brings, your goal should be to become in the top 1% of people, becoming, thus, an "Eminently Qualified Human." His inspiration came from an experience he had as a Navy Seal working with a Marine unit. One day, he watched someone fill out an evaluation form on one of his troops, where he gave his performance the highest designation and title of "Eminently Qualified Marine," meaning in the top 1%. If you strive for that high standard, it can help you with both a successful transition and enrich your life. In addition to Jocko's advice, here are a few quick tips to assist with the transition.

Find your focus. After service in the military, you must find something that has meaning for you. Consider what the new role requires and how you can apply your military experience and contribute to the overall good of the organization. Where do you get your energy? What do you enjoy doing? What do you want to learn to do?

Be humble and learn. Your expertise in the military may be unquestioned; however, you are entering a new arena. Although you may have been a highly competent military member, humbly recognize your new role will require new skills. You will likely have a steep learning curve, and you will need to spend time gaining technical, organizational, and industry knowledge. As you begin your new role, determine your gaps in knowledge and write an action plan to close the gaps.

Expect cultural communication shifts. Understand that communication will be different, so be a rapid-study student of your civilian organization's communication styles. It is OK to be a little quiet and observe others when you first start. Senior management does not have tremendous expectations of you on the first day. Take in your surroundings, watch how others communicate with one another, and observe tone and writing styles. Determine the communication norms and how they may differ from your previous experience. Adapt your personal style to a style that will help you become more effective in your non-military world.

Get comfortable with a new structure. The organization may not be as hierarchical or structured as your military experience. Although it may be more difficult to know who is actually in charge at times, recognize the value of a less-structured environment and the role it plays in your industry. Ask questions when unclear and stay disciplined and respectful to all. There is a high chance that your title, rank, and experience may have stayed in your last job in the military, and it's almost like starting from scratch in your new civilian position. That title, rank, or experience may help you get a job, but no one will ever consult you like they did when you left that last job…and you shouldn't expect it. Take the time to write down the structure and strategies to build comfort in navigating the new organization.

Add value. Get creative and find ways to contribute as early as possible. That may be by sharing new ideas or volunteering your skill sets with an organizational priority outside of your department, such as an employee group. How can you contribute to the organization's success?

Network. Although many see networking as self-serving, consider networking as an opportunity for growth as well as the chance to help others. Build authentic relationships through mutual interests and goals. Be the first to offer support, advice, or connections to your new colleagues. If they beat you to it, find ways to reciprocate. As discussed previously, never stop networking, as you may decide you want to try something new or different. Your first job out of the military may not be the right fit, and oftentimes, that is difficult to determine this until you've spent some time in the current organization. Create a networking plan.

For more information on networking, download *The Secret to Networking When You Get a New Job* at www.workplaceadvancement. com/bookclub, password nicetoknow.

Chapter 7
SUCCEEDING AS AN ENTREPRENEUR

Between 2009 – 2016, approximately 400,000
small businesses were started each year.

U.S. Chamber of Commerce

According to the U.S. Bureau of Labor Statistics, about 80 percent of small businesses successfully make it through to their first year, but only 50 percent make it to their fifth anniversary (Entrepreneur.com). Common challenges leading to business failure include entering an industry with no experience, little or no business planning, ignoring what the market really needs (therefore offering a product or service no one wants, or is saturated by existing merchants), and refusing to recognize and be flexible to changing trends. Becoming an entrepreneur is no easy task and should not be entered into without proper planning and a willingness to do whatever may become necessary for the business succeed. A look into some of the challenges and strategies of several successful entrepreneurs, working in varying product lines, can provide insight into the areas to consider before jumping into a new business start-up.

Getting Started

Working as a police officer in Atlanta, Georgia, Michael Allen Tyree realized his passion for people and safety. He grew up in New Jersey where he watched mob movies and enjoyed sports. After attending college on a basketball scholarship, he returned home, where the best employment option appeared to be working at the Stop and Shop down the street.

Michael Allen had higher aspirations, and with a belief in himself for building a stronger future, he decided to move to Atlanta, Georgia. At first, he sold cars, but he said, "I hated it. I'm not a salesman." Then, he became a police officer but said, "I always knew I wasn't a police officer by destiny."

One day, while working undercover on a train, he remembered a previous shooting on a train in France and a stabbing in London and wondered why people weren't better protected. Working undercover, he had on his bulletproof vest, but he never observed civilians wearing such protection, so he thought it must be illegal. He did his research and discovered that bulletproof vests are perfectly legal, but the ones on the market were just plain ugly! That's when Michael Allen started his pursuit to create a bulletproof vest that is more fashionable. He wanted to produce bulletproof clothing and accessories people would want to wear. His first step was the concept. The second step was selecting a unique name that would tell his story and also be memorable. He chose Thyk Skynn, took a leap of faith, and started his company. In his first two years in business, his revenues grew more than 400 percent.

Cheryl Smith also discovered a need and built a business to address it. Cheryl was in education for more than 20 years and worked as a teacher and principal before retiring. After trying several jobs, such as teaching a course or two at Indiana University, selling durable medical equipment, and working as an event planner at a local vineyard, she took a strange twist and accepted a position at a funeral home. Her role was to assist families with pre-need services and aftercare. This is where she found an unaddressed need she felt compelled to meet.

Cheryl discovered many people didn't know how to handle the barrage of activities that followed a funeral. How do you close bank accounts? What do you do with the car? What do you do with the extra furniture? So many people were hurting and at a loss as to how to best address the additional challenges that came with dealing with the estate of a loved one. That's when she decided to create Consider It Done Transition Services. She helps people going through a variety of life changes, such as kids going to college, divorce, loss of a spouse, or simply downsizing. She manages the movers, puts together furniture, and helps the owners determine what needs to be donated or sold—and then she handles it. Cheryl has a strong desire to help people and has found a unique way to support others going through life's occasionally trying times.

While thinking about a transition plan at the end of his Army service, Tyler Merritt knew he wanted to be an entrepreneur. Tyler graduated from West Point, completed flight school, and began his continuous cycle of overseas deployments. After serving as an Apache pilot in Iraq, Tyler moved to the 160th Special Operations Aviation Regiment (SOAR) unit in Savannah, Georgia (known as the "Night Stalkers"). There, he transitioned to flying Black Hawks and started his deployment cycle once again. The deployments were tough on his growing family, so he outlined a two-year transition plan from military to civilian life.

Tyler recognized a niche market for promotional products within the military community. Using his budding entrepreneurial spirit, he decided to figure out how to meet the need. He researched the shirt printing process and the equipment needed and then decided to give it a try. He and his family started the company out of his garage, and he knew right away that he was on to something. By the time he left the military two years later, Tyler's company, Nine Line Apparel, had already grown to 200 employees and approximately $25 million a year in sales.

A common beginning for each of these businesses was the owner identifying a gap in the market and creating a product or service that met the need. As you will see in this chapter, identifying the need was only the beginning. With barriers to overcome, sacrifices to make, challenges to address, a commitment to success, and a shift in mindset each was successful.

Find Your Passion

One major decision each of these owners had to make was determining if they were passionate enough about the product or service to give it their entire heart and soul. Were they willing to commit to doing whatever became necessary to make the business succeed? Running a successful business requires passion and commitment, and it rarely comes without at least some sacrifice.

Consider It Done Transition Services was born out of Cheryl's passion to help people, and she has proven to be quite good at it. Her love for people and her patience serves her well as she works with clients who are very often going through a difficult time. She may assist someone who lost a spouse and no longer needs their 5,000 square foot home and must make difficult emotional decisions about what to keep as they downsize. Or perhaps it is someone who is recently divorced and is having to make life changes, or even a college student setting up a dorm room for the first time in a distant state or city.

Cheryl genuinely loves working with people and feels that by using her educational training, she can help others reorganize their life. She said, "Basically, I am still just writing lesson plans, but this time it's for different adult life transitions. I break it into smaller chunks, realizing that there is a range of emotions all along the way."

Michael Allen shared that his motivation for Thyk Skynn was to keep people alive. He said, "I don't want to be cheated out of experiencing the range of gifts these people have to offer society. I want to be able to watch their future movies, I want to read the books they will write, and I want to go to the restaurants they may establish. I have to help keep them alive long enough so they can figure out their goals and reach their potential." After starting Thyk Skynn, Michael Allen felt he was finally doing what he was destined to do. He felt as if he found both himself and his calling. He said, "I'm finally alive."

Nine Line Apparel is not your typical apparel company. Tyler infused the company culture with his passions. He is proud of our country and our flag. He's unapologetically patriotic, and it shows in his organization. He wants to bridge the gap between civilians and service members, including veterans, law enforcement, and first responders.

Tyler's love for aircraft is obvious. A medivac helicopter representing a "Nine Line" is the core part of his logo (to soldiers, a Nine Line symbolizes patriotism, hope, and trust in one's countrymen). It is not unheard of to find a helicopter landing on the corporate property or conducting stunts to entertain the team. Tyler wants to create jobs in America, so he continually looks for ways to manufacture products here in the U.S.

As much as possible, he hires veterans, and he donates a portion of his profits to veteran needs through his Nine Line Foundation. As stated on his website, "At its core, Nine Line is a give-back organization, forever striving to be our brother's keeper, and encouraging others to do the same. We support a multitude of initiatives beyond raising awareness and financially backing organizations that help those in need. From first responders to military charities to disaster relief initiatives, Nine Line is committed to the ongoing support of charitable initiatives." Tyler feels he is definitely in his dream job and he can use his entrepreneurial spirit to build a successful apparel company that, in turn, can give back to veterans and the community.

Along with passion, entrepreneurs need commitment. Cheryl says, "You just have to stick with it once you decide." She believes everyone is an entrepreneur, but it takes total commitment to being successful.

After experiencing tough times and self-doubt, Cheryl made the conscious decision to stick it out and get more creative on her service offerings. At a time when her business was struggling and needed a boost, instead of maintaining the current strategy or outright just giving up, she added a "snowbird service" where she checks on people's homes throughout her Indiana area, while they are spending the winter in Florida. Her commitment to figuring it out, getting creative, even when it looks impossible, definitely contributed to her organizational growth.

Overcoming fear can be a huge obstacle. When Michael Allen refers to fear, it's not the fear of leaving a job or the security that a career or even a stable income provides, but for him, it is more the fear of giving people your heart and soul and having it rejected. "You give it your heart, sweat, and tears, and others don't understand the vision. They criticize your ideas. Many people can't handle that rejection, and if that's the case, entrepreneurship is not for them. You have to believe in yourself, even when others don't." Successful entrepreneurs recruit like-minded people to join them on the journey. You may not be able to pay them what they are worth, but if you have a compelling mission, others will join you. First, though, they have to see that you truly have the resolve to make it work.

Often, full commitment does lead to sacrifices. Tyler Merritt ate peanut butter and jelly sandwiches while on deployment so he could save his money for new equipment or software. He decided that he was "all in." He sold his house and moved into a smaller apartment. He and his family didn't take vacations, and holidays were often spent eating Chinese take-out while packaging products for shipment. Since the beginning, Tyler says he found himself "failing at times and even losing bunches of money." However, drawing heavily from his military training, he stated, "You have to keep on driving, and adapting, and overcoming, and finding the workarounds to whatever problems you run in to." Passion, commitment, sacrifice, and an adjustable mindset are the foundation of a successful entrepreneurial endeavor.

Turning Your Passion into A Business

Turning your passion and commitment into a business may take a mindset change and most likely will involve proactively seeking out and learning new skills. Michael Allen compared the mental shift to the difference between hunting and being fed. When we are fed, our food is provided for us. We sit at the table to eat, use a fork and knife, and follow the acceptable table manners we've been taught. When you are hunting and hungry, you drop your preconceived ideas of the accepted practices and use all resources available to secure your next meal. You look for ways to survive. You may find yourself eating with your hands, your food may be on a rock instead of a plate, and your meal may have been cooked over an open fire. At one point, he recalled thinking that a jaguar only eats deer or small game until one day he saw a video clip where the jaguar jumped in a lake and grabbed a crocodile by the neck. Michael Allen thought, "Now that's an entrepreneur!" In business, Michael Allen says, "Just because they told you something, doesn't mean that's the way it is." A hunter in the business world isn't constrained by what he is fed—just like the jaguar, he goes out and finds the "crocodile" opportunities.

According to Tyler, a big difference between entrepreneurial endeavors and regular corporate work is it's all on you. "In the military, you have that security. I've got guaranteed insurance, I've got a guaranteed paycheck, and there is less to worry about in terms of personal needs. Once you go home as an entrepreneur, a small business owner, there's no turning it off. You're always going to have those phone calls, you are always the commander, you are the one with everything at risk." You must do all that's possible to make the business successful.

Like Michael Allen, Tyler has a hunter mentality. When he goes to a restaurant and sees they are selling shirts, he will ask to talk to the manager and give them his card. When he goes to sporting events, he is networking and looking for new opportunities. He always has the company on his mind, and he is always selling.

Finding new opportunities and turning them into success will require an unrelenting pursuit of new information and new skills. Michael Allen had to learn about bulletproof vests. First, was it even legal to wear them? What is Kevlar? What type of sewing machine works with Kevlar? Where do you get it? How much does it cost? And how do you even start a business?

For Tyler, it was learning the printing process, technology, and website design and how to make the production, marketing, and selling all connect efficiently and effectively. Cheryl had a huge learning curve regarding just about everything about being in business. Basics such as registering a business with the state, creating marketing pieces, pricing services, and learning legal requirements were all new experiences for Cheryl.

Where do you go to learn these new skills? As shared in previous chapters, there are multiples avenues. Early in her business development, Cheryl sought out people who were already in business and asked about their story, their successes, and their challenges. She recalled being surprised that people were so happy to tell their story. Also, she joined a business networking group, which not only helped her learn new business skills, but also increased her actual network, which ultimately landed her one of her best referral sources. She also pursued multiple industry certifications.

When Cheryl started to write her business plan, she found free resources on the SCORE website (Senior Corps of Retired Executives, www.score.org), which included a template for writing a business plan. For entrepreneurs, SCORE can be a valuable source of information. It has many business tools available online. They also offer courses for entrepreneurs and free mentoring from successful retired executives in many industries. Best yet, in today's interconnected world, the mentors are not limited by proximity. Although Cheryl lived in Indiana, she secured a mentor from Savannah, Georgia who helped her understand her business financials and set priorities on where to focus and which metrics to track carefully. She attributes still being open for business six years later to the wise and focused support of that one key mentor.

Cheryl also learned how to apply skills she learned as an educator. She successfully transferred her lesson planning techniques and the leadership skills she acquired as a principal to her new business venture. Tyler Merritt adapted his military decision-making process, analytical skills, and emotional intelligence to help him set goals and lead his team. He learned that every human being you interact with has different motivating factors. In the military, he interacted with many different cultures and learned to find commonality among them, which was invaluable as the leader of his new organization.

Relationships

When starting a business, you may be surprised at how it changes your relationships, personally and professionally, sometimes for the better, sometimes not. Your friends and family may have different ideas regarding the risks you are taking as you start. However, you will also meet new people and build new encouraging relationships.

For Michael Allen, it was important to break stereotypes. Growing up, he says, "The only cool people in my culture rapped or played sports." Many of his relationships revolved around sports. His perception of businessmen was that they were not "cool." "There was no swag," he says, so it was not something to aspire to be. Plus, he really didn't know anyone in business.

As an athlete with multiple tattoos, he never considered the idea that he could use his mind, follow his dreams, own a business, and actually make money. "If I had known that you could earn a living by giving, I'd do it. My focus is giving of myself, my ideas, and products, not on being a salesman, but to be engaged in 'trading.' I felt like no one gets the bad end of the stick with a trade. I want to be one of the best traders ever."

On his journey to be one of the best traders ever, Michael Allen experienced the old cliché: If you want to know who your friends are, start a business. Although it was frustrating at first, Michael Allen began to understand different types of relationships. Some people will celebrate with you; they will be there in the good times. There are the family members at Christmas meals who you laugh with and enjoy their company. And then there are the family and friends who will go to "war" with you. They will support you no matter the circumstance.

He suggests that instead of getting mad at those who may not appear to be as supportive, recognize that those relationships are different. Perhaps they are not the ones cut out for the "war" you will encounter in business. Embrace the relationships for what they are. Recognize those who will go to "war" with you and be sure to show your appreciation for their unwavering support.

It is easy to get drawn into the business and forget the motivation or reason you started the business to begin with. Tyler advises new entrepreneurs to determine in advance what they want to do, how much money they need to be happy, and the lifestyle they hope to pursue. Sacrifices will be required, but, if possible, know the consequences. He says consider the question, "When I start experiencing success and get my boat, will I really need to pursue more money to get a bigger boat? Will I need a yacht? If you don't know your goals, you are just growing without an end state in mind."

Also, consider the tradeoffs you will be making to take the company to the next level. Too many entrepreneurs chase growth and greater wealth at the expense of their family and friends. When this became a concern for Tyler, he realized, "It's about making memories and finding the time to enjoy life with your co-workers and with your family members and finding and maintaining that work-life balance." Now, recognizing the need for balance, and to ensure he has quality time with his children, he bought an RV and takes his children with him on the road.

Cheryl cautions not to overburden family members with business concerns. Unless your family is in business with you, they may have some interest in your operation, but they will not be as invested as you are. For the sake of the relationship, you both need the separation. However, you will need to be able to share your concerns, your frustrations, your challenges, and your successes with someone. She said, "You need someone you can just go to no matter what. It might be a family member. But for me, I draw the line and rely on someone outside of the family."

In addition to having a strong friend to rely on, Cheryl recommends building lots of new relationships. It is important to build a relationship with your accountant, your banker, and your lawyer. Check out your local Chamber of Commerce and take advantage of their seminars and networking events. Build relationships with people in your industry. Many business sectors have national organizations where you can meet people from different regions and learn new trends and best practices. Through her national association, Cheryl has met and developed relationships with colleagues from Pennsylvania to California who have turned out to be great resources. And with technology today, geography isn't a barrier.

There Will Be Challenges Along the Way

A common challenge for a growing business owner is to know when to get out of the "weeds" or the nitty-gritty details. Cheryl recognized she had a hard time letting go. After she gained an understanding of fundamental business practices, she tended to stay involved in the details. She finally recognized that, although she needed to know enough to understand the business, she had access to accountants and lawyers to help with the details. She needed to let them do it. However, when it came to operations and her staff, it was difficult for her not to be involved in even the smallest of decisions. It was some of her colleagues who helped her to see that staying involved in the day-to-day general operational decisions was holding her and her company back from growth opportunities.

Tyler admitted that he too had difficulty staying out of the minutia. He stated, "If I walked by and saw something that was out of the standards, even something minor, I would stop right there and correct it, right then." Once he realized he should be working "on the business," not "in the business," his focus changed. He said, "I'm hemorrhaging tens of thousands of dollars, but I'm focused on this widget that costs fifty cents." The little things became distractions from the bigger picture. He learned to rely on his leadership team to focus on the day-to-day operations, while he focused on growing the business. And that, of course, means hiring the right people.

For Thyk Skynn, Michael Allen went back to his hunting analogy. If you are hunting and you are hungry, you feel it physically and you know you are hungry. In business, you may have money in the bank and think you are just fine. Then, you realize you have $5,000 in the bank, but you owe $20,000 in overhead. "Now you are starving to death and you didn't feel it!" That's the danger of staying too focused on the small things and not being sufficiently aware of the bigger picture. Your organization can be in danger of "starvation," but you may not see it until it's too late.

Making it Through the Tough Times

As with any business, there are going to be tough times, some expected and some not. Business owners recommend remembering the "why" of your business and keeping a sense of humor. Many of Cheryl's clients will tell her she can keep anything she wants out of their possessions. Typically, she has spent time with them and heard their stories about their items and their special significance. If it is someone Cheryl has worked with for a long time, she may carefully select a small item that was to be donated to Goodwill and will keep it as a reminder of the client to help her remember the "why."

Cheryl recalled one client who was hard to forget. She was helping a sweet lady move several items, including a loom that was to be donated to the Smithsonian Institute. While they were marking items to be moved or donated, they came upon a beautiful dresser and the client stated, "I think it's all empty." As she opened one of the doors, a prosthetic arm fell out! The client simply stated, "Oh, that's just my husband" and tossed it. When Cheryl went back for the move, she was pleased to discover the arm was gone. However, at Christmas time, her staff presented Cheryl with a beautifully wrapped gift. And as she opened it, the entire team laughed hysterically. Yes, Cheryl had "the husband," or at least his arm!

Michael Allen also found some humor in his business success. He stated, "I never knew that so many women were attracted to an entrepreneur." There seems to be an attraction to the "hunters." He always thought being a businessman would be lonely, but he found that once you make things happen, he says, "You ain't lonely anymore!"

Recognizing that humor won't be the answer in every situation, Cheryl suggests taking a breath and taking your time. There are situations where you need to simply step away and take about 24 hours to let it marinate. Everything doesn't need a reaction immediately. During that time, consider what you don't know about the situation and ask for more information, before too aggressively correcting the concern.

Recommended Action Steps from Those Who Went Before You

Be passionate and disciplined. Creating a successful business is up to you, and it takes discipline. Each of the entrepreneurs interviewed shared the need to set goals and include measurements that recognize progress towards the goals. It is easy to get sidetracked with a new "shiny object," but staying focused and disciplined in everyday operations contributes to organizational success. Is there an area where you have difficulty focusing? What strategies will you put in place to help you stay disciplined and focused?

Balance passion and dreams with business numbers. Michael Allen cautions that it is easy to get caught up in your passion and lose sight of the numbers. He attributes some of his success to his ability to both dream and to understand the numbers. Understanding the numbers, and paying attention to them, helps to keep a balance between dreams and reality. What do you need to learn? Do you understand accounting? Do you understand balance sheets? If not, write down a plan to obtain the business tracking skills you will need to be successful.

Build relationships and create a personal board of directors. Cheryl sought out people she could rely on to help her with encouragement and expertise. Being intentional regarding developing her small group, Cheryl found people with marketing expertise, a great accountant, and industry experts. She recommends not being shy about building relationships and seeking out the help you need. Take a few minutes to write out the areas where you could benefit from the expertise of others. In what areas might that be? Consider who you know with those skills.

They may be industry colleagues, business owners, retired executives, and even friends, neighbors, or family members.

Be intentional about your business culture. No matter what business you start or where you compete, your culture can be a differentiator. Use it to your benefit. As Tyler discovered, there is a large market for people who have the same desire to support first responders and veterans and to give back to the community. Not only is it evident in his products, but he was also purposeful in building a company culture that is congruent with his products. What does your ideal business culture look like? How will you infuse your mission in everyday operations? How will you engrain your desired culture into your team? Make developing a company and team cultural plan part of your business strategy.

Hire quality employees. Quality people will deliver results during tough times. Tyler found that having quality people in every role in his business made a huge difference. They bring innovative ideas, and in his case, many of them have a military background and intuitively understand the mission and vision. What does your ideal employee look like? What values do they have that will support your mission? Where will you find the right people? Be intentional about your recruitment and management plan. With the right people, you are better prepared for success and to address new challenges.

Ready to start your own business? Check out our Entrepreneur Quiz *Do You Have What It Takes To Start Your Own Business?* Access the quiz at www.workplaceadvancement.com/bookclub, password nicetoknow.

Chapter 8
RETIREMENT

"In the United States, approximately
10,000 people turn 65 each day."

(Guillaume Vandenbroucke)

With thousands of people turning 65 each day, there are a lot of people in the United States who are either retired or contemplating when they will retire. When most people do plan for retirement, they primarily consider their financial situation to determine what lifestyle they can afford. However, there is much more to consider. Retirement can redefine your lifestyle, and, possibly, redefine you. When envisioning your retirement picture, questions to consider include the following:

- What do you value?
- How will your role with your family and friends change?
- What will be the impact on your identity, social life, and personal fulfillment?

Retirement life has been redefined in the past several years to offer many options, and the right option varies by individual. Today, it is rare that someone works for only one employer and then completely retires at age 62 or even age 65. Some people easily transition from the world of work to a retirement life, where they spend more time with family, traveling, or enjoying the hobbies and interests that were not easily pursued while working. Others may choose to volunteer with an organization that provides a sense of meaning and purposeful work. Still others may begin a "second act," starting a job that moves them in an entirely new direction, and others may never plan to officially retire. This chapter shares the stories, struggles, and advice from happy retirees who each took a different path that met their needs while providing the fulfillment they were seeking.

First Question, Who Am I?

Ginger Jennings worked in sales for many years at the number one network affiliate television station in Savannah, Georgia. She asked friends, "How do you know when it is time to retire?" and repeatedly was told, "You will just know." Then she asked a friend, "What do you do" (in retirement)?" Her friend responded, "Anything you want to do!"

Although her career was at a high point, Ginger decided it was time to retire. Just two short months after retiring, she was reading a book and started feeling guilty. She kept thinking there must have been something she was supposed to be doing other than enjoying a book.

The transition from work to being able to do whatever she wanted to do was difficult, and it took for her time to adjust, so she could give herself the freedom to do the things she wanted to do guiltfree. Although reading a book was something she wanted to do, she kept feeling as if there was something else she "needed" to do. For someone who had worked her entire adult life, it took time for her to enjoy her newfound freedom, until she realized she now had the opportunity to travel and spend more time with friends and family.

Like many people who contemplate retirement, a good portion of

Michael Siegel's identity was based on what he did professionally. After spending much of his career as a chief information officer in several organizations, Michael decided to move into consulting. From that point, his transition to retirement was gradual.

Ultimately, after 40 years in the professional world, he transitioned from consulting to actual retirement, but he struggled with his identity and how he would redefine himself. A close friend gave him this advice: "You have to learn how to be a UTBI." Not understanding the term "UTBI," Michael asked for clarification, at which point his friend responded, "Used To Be Important!" Michael recognized the truth in that statement and laughed, but then decided he wanted to find a way to do something that gave him a purpose, something where he could contribute and do some good. Volunteerism was a natural option.

After 27 years of federal service, to include serving as a helicopter pilot flying Cobras in the Army and as an air traffic controller with the FAA, Bob Snuck decided to retire. He knew he still had a lot of interests to pursue, and he even had a strong desire to continue working. Early in his life, Bob built homes on the side and developed an interest in real estate, so after retiring from the government, he obtained his real estate license and started his own business. Though the real estate business was successful, he soon realized it was not his passion. After only a few years, he decided to sell his business. He then found the opportunity to become, of all things, a train conductor. He really thought that would be interesting, and indeed, he did enjoy it. This role allowed him to see the country from an entirely different point of view. However, again he realized it was not his passion.

After leaving federal service, Bob had tried many different professions but eventually realized through his varied experiences that his passion was aviation. While at the FAA, he had maintained his flight status and worked with several private charter companies, sometimes flying celebrities, including Paul Newman and Katharine Hepburn. Although he did enjoy flying, he wanted to pursue another aspect of the aviation field. He returned to school and earned a master's degree in business administration. Then, with degree in hand, he went on to earn an airport management certification from the American Association of Airport Executives, which led to several jobs managing small airports around the nation. Experimenting in roles after he retired allowed Bob the opportunity to discover how to best continue to apply his talents and passion in the field that he had loved all along.

During his 20-year career as a pilot in the United States Air Force, Jack Scoggins became known as an extraordinary pilot and earned multiple medals, including two Distinguished Flying Crosses in combat while serving as a rescue pilot in Vietnam. After his wartime service, Jack was assigned to assist with post-launch rocket and astronaut retrieval for Apollo 17 and four Sky Lab launches. Following his extensive time in the Air Force, Jack joined two other men and started Air Valdosta, located in Valdosta, Georgia, where he taught flying lessons and managed the flight school.

At age 79, and still flying, the FAA awarded Jack the Wright Brothers "Master Pilot" Award for more than 60 years of safe flying experience. Then at age 84, while still flying and instructing students, Jack was recognized as the "Flight Instructor of the Year" by the Georgia Aviation Hall of Fame. At the time of this book interview, Jack was 90, had passed the physical examinations and other requirements to maintain his flight status, and was still flying! He never questioned his career identity. He knew he was, and will always be, a pilot. His love for flying started early in life. He obtained his pilot's license at the age of 19 and has never stopped flying. When asked his thoughts on retirement, he simply responded, "I am going to teach as long as I'm able."

Freedom!

When asked about retirement, a common response was "freedom." Freedom to do the things you've always wanted to do, with less stress. Ginger Jennings stated that when she was working, she did not realize how busy she was and how totally work-centered her life had become. She recalled a time when she was on her way to call on a client, thinking about that upcoming meeting, but remembering that she needed to cash a check. She stopped at the drive-through lane at the bank, cashed her check, and headed to her client's office. It was then that she suddenly realized she still had the bank's drive-through canister still in her car.

She looks back now and doesn't know how she fit everything in. With her new freedom in retirement, she met new "gal" friends to, as she put it, "play with." She now has more friends with diverse interests. She spends time with her lady pals going to the movies. She has her fitness-focused clan and a group that likes to go to lunch. Yet another group likes to travel. Ginger is also enjoying more time with her family. Now, she can be the first one at her grandchildren's shows, pick them up for lunch, or take them for a quick trip to the store. Her advice is to use your new freedom wisely. Get out of your house and out of your comfort zone, try new experiences, and especially, as she has done, expand your relationships. Most importantly, she urges new retirees to take negativity and stress out of their life. Remove the drama and focus on the positive. Her mantra is, "Life is wonderful, so make it wonderful."

Michael Siegel agrees that retirement provides you with more opportunities to pursue the things you want to do. "For the most part, you can do what you want, as much as you want, when you want," he says. Michael believes having more control over your time allows you to focus your time and talent in a positive way. "I believe that anything you do in retirement, whatever it is, should be two things. It should be fulfilling, and it should be fun. And if you're doing something that isn't fulfilling or fun, you need to find something else to do."

Plan Before You Retire

Know your current financial status and overall predictive financial picture. The type of life you live in retirement will be dramatically impacted by your financial means. Ginger spent time with her financial counselor asking for a realistic projection of when, based on her preferred retirement lifestyle, it made sense to retire. She surrounded herself with people who knew more than she did and who could help navigate her path.

In addition to financial counseling, Ginger recommends understanding your insurance needs, speaking with an attorney regarding your legal affairs, and staying in touch with your banker. Also, remember to talk with friends who have already retired. She learned about many senior discounts through friends and now when making plans or purchases, she consistently asks if they offer a senior discount.

According to Michael, it is important to plan long before you "ride off into the sunset." He started involving himself in volunteer activities a year or more before he stepped out of his consulting practice, making the transition much easier. He had friends who decided to retire without much of a plan on how they would spend their time. When all of the sudden the emails stopped, the phone calls stopped, and they were sitting at home, they were not sure what to do. By identifying early on that he wanted to stay involved with people and experimenting with what that may entail prior to retirement, Michael was able to find a shorter path to redefining himself going forward.

Bob knew he wanted to continue to work after retirement. For roles that were of interest to him, Bob conducted internet searches to identify the job requirements. Then, he would create his "checklist" and begin preparing himself to be a strong candidate for the role. He found that he had to be willing to take a step back. For him, that meant starting at smaller airports where he could gain experience and learn new skills required for running an airport.

Now, as he considers "full" retirement soon, he is planning on building an airplane. To that desired end, he is spending time researching home-built airplane options and applicable federal regulations and guidelines. Taking the time to plan not only the financial considerations but also how you will use your time, will create a smoother transition from work to "your time."

Continue to Use Your Skills!

One of Michael's retirement goals is to "die with an empty head." He knows he has a lot of knowledge to share, and he wants to give it all away! This goal drove his retirement planning. He worked hard to find a way to reinvent himself while still adding value. Moving from the corporate world to consulting, Michael realized he could live anywhere and decided he wanted to determine where that would be. He fell in love with Savannah, Georgia, while working for a large medical center earlier in his career and decided to return there. It was in Savannah where his passion for volunteerism began to bloom.

Having a master's degree in marine biology, Michael started volunteering for the University of Georgia Marine Education Center and Aquarium. This allowed him to share his formal education by teaching children about Coastal Georgia, while finding a new way to contribute his expertise. He recalled one rewarding experience, when he observed that a little boy was absorbed with one of the aquarium's "touch tanks" full of hermit crabs. Michael recalled saying to him, "Come on bud, we have to go down to the other aquarium." At that point, the little boy ran over, hugged Michael's leg, and, looking up, said, "Will you be my bud?" It touched Michael deeply, and he realized it was an experience that would never happen in the corporate world. Although it was a totally different type of fulfillment, Michael was on his way to finding his identity and new purpose and another way of "emptying his head."

In addition to volunteering at the Marine Education Center, Michael began volunteering in his congregation, led a photography club, and became a mentor with SCORE providing free business mentoring services to aspiring entrepreneurs and small business owners, all of which used his leadership skills. It was SCORE that provided him the opportunity to use the skills he gained over the years, and ultimately, he became the chapter chair.

Michael noted, "My experience at SCORE allows me to share my knowledge with people new to business who are looking for help. It allows me to leverage my organizational and team-building skills. It allows me to develop fundraising skills that I never had before. And, through SCORE, I've met so many incredible people all over the city and county. You develop friends and friendships, through knowledge sharing." It all has helped him get one step closer to his goal of "dying with an empty head."

Although Jack has a degree in mechanical engineering, he continues to learn and incorporate a lifetime of knowledge into his daily routine. Early in his Air Force career, he became accustomed to the requirement that he learn new skills. Every time he moved into a new position or learned to fly a new aircraft, he had extensive training. Before leaving the Air Force, he studied to become a certified civilian flight instructor and later became certified as a helicopter instructor pilot. Ultimately, he was designated as a pilot examiner by the FAA. When asked to distinguish between teaching military pilots and teaching civilians, he said, "That is easy. In the military, you do the training, or you are out. With civilians, you have to motivate them to do things."

He recalled a particular conversation where he told a student he needed to learn how to do crosswind landings or forward slips to landing, but the student wasn't interested. The student said, "Well, I'll never use that. I don't have to learn how to do it because I don't plan on doing it." Jack responded, "So, you don't plan on having an emergency?" With Jack's lifetime of experience flying and recognition for his safety record, he knew the importance of planning for an emergency and staying updated on equipment and any new information in the field of aviation. He feels so strongly about continuous learning that it is not uncommon for Jack to sign up for classes on engine maintenance or other areas of interest related to aircraft and flight instruction. He has even been known to read aviation accident reports while vacationing on a cruise!

Enjoy Life and Stay Engaged

For personal fulfillment, as well as for your health, stay active. Whether you spend time with friends or start a new career in your retirement, you will need to stay involved, keep your mind active, and build a strong social network. Stress and loneliness can have a negative impact on your health. As such, it is advantageous to stay active as an aid to good mental and physical health. Michael recommends looking for activities in retirement as passionately as you did when you were looking for a job. Your job now is to discover the activities that are right and most helpful and healthful for you.

- Are there activities you think you might enjoy that you previously did not have time to pursue?
- Do you want to learn to play golf or simply play more golf?
- Tennis anyone?
- Are you interested in taking a painting class?
- Do you enjoy photography?
- Are there travel destinations you had hoped to visit?
- Is there a skill or further schooling you want to accomplish?

As mentioned before, after retiring from federal service, Bob went back to school and completed his MBA, which he found to be quite valuable when he managed airports. With a background in aviation, plus formal business training, he was able to help small airports become more efficient and financially viable, providing him with a great sense of satisfaction and fulfillment.

Several resources are available in most communities to help you learn new skills, engage in new experiences, and broaden your social network. One often-overlooked resource is a community senior center. They may offer educational lectures, courses on different hobbies, or exercise classes.

Colleges and universities typically allow seniors to audit courses free of charge. At one point after leaving the Air Force, Jack participated in a Russian Art History class offered by his local university. However, he cautions, you need to fully understand what may be expected. His class was taught in Russia, so it involved travel and living in college accommodations.

It took Ginger Jennings about 8-9 months to reinvent herself and figure out how she wanted to stay engaged. Although she no longer had to get up at 5:30 am to get ready and head to work, it was a long time before she was able to break that decades-long habit. She is an outgoing person and wanted to stay connected with people, so she knew she needed to find a balance between any future commitments and being certain to make time for herself.

She wanted to do something that made her feel good about herself, while providing social interaction. To those ends, she got more involved with her favorite charity, the Ronald McDonald House. As she planned for retirement, she had determined she did not want to work. However, her friends and previous clients kept encouraging her to create her own advertising agency. Reluctantly, she took on a few clients and commented that, "It helped me keep my thumb in the pie, while still balancing everything else I want to do." It also provided her with social interaction, kept her engaged in the work she loved, and provided her with a sense of purpose in retirement.

Building a social network is vitally important. At age 83, Jack was rushed to a hospital two hours from his home due to a serious medical emergency. While Jack was in ICU, his wife of 49 years passed due to a heart attack. Many people thought as a decorated war veteran, a fulfilling career, and the loss of his wife, Jack might give up. Even though he was hospitalized in ICU, his condition serious, and the outcome appearing grim, Jack was determined to make it back home. Against all odds, and to the surprise of many in the medical community, he did make it home and continued his recuperation. It was during that time that he and his family more fully realized the value of a strong network.

Before the incident, Jack had long-term relationships with many of the pilots he had trained, met with his Air Force buddies weekly for coffee, participated in a weekly informal men's coffee time with other friends, enjoyed spending time with neighbors and coworkers, and was active in his church. In addition to Jack's strong will, it was the support of each of these groups, as well as many others, that encouraged him through his health challenge and ultimately, contributed to his successful recovery. At age 90, he continues to remain active and in good health. Best of all, he now has a lovely new bride!

Recommended Action Steps from Those Who Went Before You

First question, who am I? Know Yourself. Ginger knew she wanted to spend time with friends and family. Michael knew he was good with people and want to continue to engage with others while contributing to his community. Bob wanted to pursue brand new roles and challenges, and Jack wanted to continue his life-long passion for flying. Determine what motivates you. What makes you happy? Is there a part of your career that you want to continue to pursue after your formal retirement? Is there something entirely new that you want to pursue? Capture your thoughts and aspirations on paper and perhaps even share them with your family.

Embrace freedom! Retirement provides you with more opportunities to pursue the things you want to do. You have more control over your time, and you can focus your time and talents in new, fulfilling ways. Spend time considering how you will spend your new freedom!

Plan before you retire. Define yourself outside of work. Begin to let go of how you thought of yourself in the past and focus on this new chapter in your life. Consider how daily routines may change. What do you want these new routines to entail? How might retirement impact your family and friends? What are their expectations of this new relationship with them? How will the roles and responsibilities at home change? Discuss your thoughts with your family and develop a plan that works for everyone close to you.

Continue to use your skills. Whether it be with your family, a community organization, a new business, or some combination of all three, determine ways to contribute that are pleasing and meaningful to you. The more you can incorporate your skills and passions into your retirement lifestyle, the more rewarding it will be.

Enjoy life and stay engaged. Start transitioning before you retire. "Be sure you are going toward something, not just away from something," cautioned Michael. Start getting involved in some of your desired retirement activities before you retire. If it's more time with family, begin spending some more time with them now. If you want to volunteer, but are not sure where, contact your local United Way or check out www.volunteermatch. com. There are volunteer opportunities everywhere. If you plan on starting a new business, check out the resources at SCORE. Their experienced business experts can help you develop a sound and comprehensive plan. However, realize as with any change, it will take time to get accustomed to your new reality. The individual time frame varies based on multiple elements, so there is no hard and fast rule regarding how long it will take for you to get comfortable with the post-work "new you!"

Still looking for things to do? Download 25 Things to Do After Your Well-Earned Retirement at www.workplaceadvancement.com/ bookclub, password nicetoknow.

WHAT'S NEXT?

"Information is not knowledge. The only
source of knowledge is experience."

Albert Einstein

Sincere thanks for purchasing, and more importantly, reading this book. I trust you found the experiences and advice shared in each chapter to be insightful and that you have found a way to apply the material to enhance and advance your career. Even though the interviews were with people in different career stages, and with vastly different work environments, a few common trends emerged and are worth noting when you make a career change. Most importantly, your success is up to you.

Know yourself. It is OK to recognize that you cannot be perfect at everything. Understand your strengths and how they can be beneficial to the new organization. Be honest with yourself, even before you make a change. Take personality inventories and self-assessment quizzes and ask for feedback, with the intent of gaining a better understanding of yourself. Throughout your career, take assignments and roles that may leverage your strengths and help you become a strong contributor quickly.

Know the industry. Join industry email threads. Most industries have organizations that provide updated information on their specific sector. Research articles, journals, blogs, and other sources that provide updates and trends. Some information may be posted daily, and other information may be posted routinely but less frequently. It is a great way to stay informed on emerging trends while growing your knowledge base.

Adapt your communication style. Even before you start your new role, you can gain insight into the organization's communication style. Review the website, recruitment material, emails, and any other communications you receive from the organization. Look for hints as to their culture and communication style. Know that it is OK to be a little quiet at first. Senior management typically does not have tremendous expectations of you on the very first day. Try to take in your surroundings, watch how others communicate with one another, and observe tone and writing styles. Determine communication norms and how they may differ from your previous experience. Adapt your style to one that will help you become the most effective.

Be positive. Not only is it important that you are positive about your current role, but discussions regarding previous roles and teams also need to stay positive. Write down a few actions that can help you stay upbeat. Will you keep a journal of the good things that make you happy at your place of employment? Will you subscribe to a blog that encourages positivity? Will you focus on the positive aspects of your role during your quiet time? Will you hang out with positive people? Be intentional and specific with your positivity plan.

Ask for help. As with any new role, it is important to seek the help you need. Even if you come with extensive experience, it is tempting to move forward as if the things that made you successful elsewhere will work in your new role. That might not always be the case. You may need to adapt your skills and learn new ones. Take the time to observe the organization, learn the culture, and ask a lot of questions. If you are unsure, ask for the help you need, thereby demonstrating a willingness to learn and building solid relationships and trust with the team more quickly.

Remember the basics. An immediate contribution you can make is to ensure that you continue with basic professional behaviors. As before, show up to your job on time or early and wear appropriate attire. Stay sharp and alert and pay attention to the little things. You are expected to not only be punctual but prepared to get right to work and deliver timely results. Set a strong example of commitment from the beginning and recognize that you are not only doing the job you were hired to do but also enhancing your career reputation.

Build relationships. Build strong relationships at every level in the organization. Ask for suggestions of people throughout the organization whom you should meet. That includes, of course, people in the department you will need to work with on projects, people who are the best at a particular skill, and people who understand the politics of the organization. Seek out top performers across departments as well as leaders from multiple disciplines within your organization. Proactively set up meetings with them to learn their perspective and what is known to contribute to success.

Gain clarity. Meet with your manager early to learn the strategic value of your role and the organization's short- and long-term expectations of you. Create a plan for what you hope to accomplish in the first 30, 60, and 90 days. Consider your transferable skills and how you can add value immediately. Compare your manager's expectations of you in the same 30, 60, and 90-day timeframes and create an agreed-upon plan with goals that align with the overall organizational strategy.

Learn from your mistakes. Expect to make mistakes, as most people new to any job do. The environment is new, and you will not be perfect. Pick yourself up and keep going. Consider what happened and what you might do differently if that situation arises again. Create a learning log to capture your observations. Also, if possible, find a colleague, an "encouragement partner," who can help you move on, and most importantly, grow!

As a special gift for those who have purchased this book, I have a section on my website with additional free resources that can be easily accessed at **www.workplaceadvancement.com/bookclub, password nicetoknow.**

Resources include:

- Brand Building Worksheet
- Work From Home Survey
- Leadership Style Quiz
- 10 Important Qualities for Leadership at Work
- Resilience: 7 Skills You Need to Succeed during a Transition Checklist
- Secret to Networking When You Get A New Job
- Do You Have What It Takes To Start Your Own Business Quiz
- 25 Things to Do After Your Well-Earned Retirement

I would love to stay in touch and learn how you have successfully navigated your career transition. Please send me a quick note at julieolsen@workplaceadvancement.com and say hello, share your story, and offer advice or tips that may benefit others. Best of luck as you continue to advance personally and professionally!

NOTES

Introduction

Belli, Gina (2019) Are you job hopping too much? https://www.pay-scale.com/career-news/2019/04/are-you-job-hopping-too-much

Bureau of Labor Statistics, U.S. Department of Labor, Employee Tenure Summary 2018 https://www.bls.gov/news.release/tenure.nr0.htm

Hyman, Jeff (2019). The number one reason people fail in new roles (It's not what you think). https://www.forbes.com/sites/jeffhyman/2019/02/21/dna/?sh=4e22d47c1805

Chapter 1

Oakes, Kevin. (2012) How long does it take to get fully productive? Training Industry Quarterly. https://www.nxtbook.com/nxtbooks/trainingindustry/tiq_2012winter/index.php?startid=40#/p/40

Chapter 3

Oracle (2019) New Study: 64% of people trust a robot more than their manager. https://www.prnewswire.com/news-releases/new-study-64-of-people-trust-a-robot-more-than-their-manager-300938324.html

Chapter 4

U.S. Bureau of Labor Statistics. National longitudinal surveys. (2020) https://www.bls.gov/nls/questions-and-answers.htm#anch44

Chapter 6

Transitioning Service Members: Information on military employment assistance centers. (2019) https://www.gao.gov/products/gao-19-438r

Parker, K, Igielnik,R., Barroso, A., Cilluffo, A. (2019). The American veteran experience and the post-9/11 generation. Pew Research Center. https://www.pewresearch.org/social-trends/2019/09/10/the-america n-veteran-experience-and-the-post-9-11-generation/

Augustine, A. Do you dread networking? Here's why it's time to change your perspective. https://www.topresume.com/career-advice/importanc e-of-networking-for-career-success

Casciaro, T., Gino, F., Kouchaki, M. (2016). Learn to love net-working. Harvard Business Review. https://hbr.org/2016/05/ learn-to-love-networking

Willink, J. (2020). The code. The evaluation. the protocols: Striving to become an eminently qualified human. Jocko Publishing.

Chapter 7

Carter, T. (2021). The true failure rate of small businesses. Entrepreneur. https://www.entrepreneur.com/article/361350

ACKNOWLEDGMENTS

First, to my amazing husband who not only encouraged me to write this book, but willingly spent hours reviewing the first draft and providing valuable recommendations and edits. Thank you for believing in me and encouraging me throughout this entire process.

To Chip Scholz, thank you for your professional encouragement, for providing valuable feedback on the composition and framework for the book, and for writing the foreword. A big thanks goes to my editor, Shannon GaNun, for providing her professional expertise and guidance for this book.

Thank you to the interesting people, friends, and family who willingly shared their experiences and advice for the book: Ali Hobbs, Nardo Govan, Jessica Olsen, Andy Cabistan, Lauren Olsen, Nick Oji, Ilona Curry, Alex Crocker, Stephanie Lamar, Stratton Leopold, Karl Diffenderfer, Brandon Ferrara, Stacy Jennings, Lisa Shumate, Kim Barnhill, Honor Lind, Bill Golden, John Wheeler, Lonnie Harrison, Brantley Player, Ken Harrison, Michael Allen Tyree, Cheryl Smith, Tyler Merritt, Ginger Jennings, Michael Siegel, Bob Snuck, and Jack Scoggins. In addition, thanks to more than 110 healthcare leaders who shared their experiences through confidential surveys and interviews.

Thanks to Marjorie Young and Deb Thompson for introducing me to successful people with great stories. I'm grateful to my friends, neighbors, and clients who encouraged me throughout the entire book writing experience, helping me move from idea to completion. Thanks to Bunny Ware and Paul Camp for a beautiful author photo. And a big thanks to each of you who read this book, you were my inspiration.

ABOUT THE AUTHOR

Dr. Julie Olsen is an experienced coach and consultant providing unique solutions and engaging leadership workshops across the country. Her passion is equipping leaders and enhancing interpersonal and team communications. Drawing from more than 30 years of comprehensive operational and leadership development experience, Dr. Olsen has helped individuals, teams, and numerous organizations advance their mission and feel more valued by leveraging their strengths. Along with her doctorate, she has earned an MBA and holds several HR certifications. She is the founder and president of Workplace Advancement Strategies. To learn more, visit www.workplaceadvancement.com.

Made in the USA
Columbia, SC
17 October 2021